TAPPED OUT

THE COMING WORLD CRISIS IN WATER AND WHAT WE CAN DO ABOUT IT

PAUL SIMON

WELCOME RAIN   New York

Tapped Out: the Coming World Crisis in Water and What We Can Do About It

by Dr. Paul Simon

First Welcome Rain paperback edition: November 2001.

First published in hardcover in the U.S. by Welcome Rain Publishers.
Tapped Out is published in association with
National Press Books of Washington, DC.

ISBN 1-56649-221-1

Printed in the United States of America.

1 3 5 7 9 10 8 6 4 2

DEDICATED TO

SHIMON PERES,

WHO KNOWS BOTH THE

IMPORTANCE OF WATER AND THE

NEED FOR BUILDING A WORLD

OF GREATER

PEACE AND UNDERSTANDING

CONTENTS

INTRODUCTION

This introduction to the paperback edition comes at a time when the issue of water is even more pressing than when I completed the manuscript three and a half years ago. Some positive things have happened since the original publication, but as we walk forward in the necessary direction, the problems are leaping forward. Unless there are intensified efforts by the United States and other nations—as well as the private sector—we face a grim future.

When the peace talks in the Middle East were going relatively smoothly, former Soviet President Mikhail Gorbachev made a speech in the Netherlands in which he said he had just been to the Middle East and met with then-Israeli Prime Minister Ehud Barak, Chairman Arafat of the Palestinian Authority, and King Abdullah of Jordan. The three leaders believed that even if all parties agreed to a peace compact, the Middle East would explode in ten years over the issue of water unless constructive answers to this overwhelming problem were found. The headline "In West Bank, Water Is as Touchy as Land" typifies more and more of the stories that cross my desk. There cannot be a dry peace in the Middle East.

Turkey and Syria came close to conflict over the use of water in two rivers that flow from Turkey into Syria. President Mubarak of Egypt flew to the area to calm things and work out an agreement, but that still has the potential to explode. So do many other areas of the world. California's water problems are starting to compound, and Texas has been warned to plan on reducing per capita water consumption by twenty-five percent in the next two decades. A few months after the hardbound edition of this book appeared in 1998, Governors Jim Edgar of Illinois and Tom Ridge of Pennsylvania invited me to speak at a meeting of Great Lakes governors and their key staffs about the future of the Great Lakes. I told them that unless answers are found for the water problems of the southwestern United States, inevitably there will be great pressure on the U.S. and Canada to share this rich water resource with our southern neighbors in need.

The Southwest is not alone. A newspaper headline notes: "Alabama, Florida and Georgia Fight Crucial Water War." They do not "fight" literally, of course, but even in the water-rich United States we will see more and more headlines like this. And problems in the United States are small compared to other nations' difficulties.

Late in 2000, U.S. intelligence agencies (including the CIA) provided a view of what the world might be like in fifteen years and the challenges we may face. One of their not-too-surprising conclusions: The world will be threatened by wars over water. How much attention did the report get? Almost none. I saw one story at the bottom of a back page in *The New York Times* but nothing anywhere else.

When an unusually capable and alert woman with responsibilities at NBC television approached me and said they would be interested in any story ideas I might have, I told her, "I have one. I'll write to you." I sent her a letter and this book. She tried to sell it to the top people at NBC, but as she told me in a phone conversation, "We're in a ratings war, and right now the subject of water doesn't have much sex appeal. It won't help our ratings." This is a condensation of what she told me, and I don't mean to pick on NBC, but it is an accurate representation of what she said. Mention the water issue to key media people and they agree on its importance, but unfortunately they also agree there is not much public interest. Unless public interest is stirred, we will face serious crises and wars that could be avoided. Creative media people ought to be able to find a "hook" that can rivet public attention—and maybe even improve ratings. Being irresponsible shouldn't be a prerequisite for higher ratings.

When speaking to groups, if I mention that 9,500 children die every day due to poor quality water, it barely gets their attention. It is only when I add that this number is 630 times as many as the number of students who were killed at Columbine High School in Colorado that audience members suddenly fall silent. Columbine High School's tragedy gripped us—as it should have—but when so many more children die unremarkably around the globe because of water-related diseases, we pay no attention. This number—9,500—is one-fourth more than the number who were killed in the tragic events of September 11, 2001, and yet we hardly take note of this larger, daily figure.

Around the world, using the mechanism of increased prices to encourage conservation is still much too rare. Even in my local water district in rural southern Illinois I pay $12.00 if I use 1,000 gallons of water in a month, and $9.00 for each 1,000 gallons after that. The international situation is getting tighter as populations grow and water sources do not; poor quality water only compounds the problem. A front-page story in *The New York Times* noted, "Part of northern China is gradually turning into desert." Another article told of Natalia Choccna Flores, a four-year-old in Peru "who tells a public health official that she has diarrhea. Natalia, with her three siblings, two dogs and a goat in tow, leads the nurse to the place where she went to the bathroom-directly in front of the family's water tank."

I recently visited a small village in Mali in Africa and saw the primitive sewer disposal right next to one of the two village wells. The average life span in Mali is 46 years. Bangladesh is plagued by arsenic in its water that causes skin lesions and is probably responsible in part for a shortened life span in that nation. A *New Yorker* profile of the Ganges river noted that in the holy city of Varanasi where many devout Hindus bathe, "the fecal count has been known to reach a hundred and seventy million bacteria per hundred milliliters of water—a terrifying three hundred and forty thousand times the acceptable level of five hundred per hundred milliliters."

But the picture is not all bleak. There are people who read the hardcover edition of this book and have become activists. Mildred Howie of Rohnert Park, California, has become zealous on this issue, and supplies me with newspaper articles about water from that state. William Sornborger, who runs a small manufacturing company in California that makes nothing relating directly to water, is taking an interest. Floyd Wicks, the enlightened C.E.O. of American States Water, is taking a leadership role, not simply because his company is involved in water development, but also because he understands where the world is headed. These three examples of responsible citizenship are people who live in California, where there is greater sensitivity to the issue.

A highly respected television documentary producer, Jim Thebaut, is exploring the possibility of doing a TV series under the title, "Running Dry." PBS ran one series about water that unfortunately received far too little attention. ITT Industries is producing a guidebook on global water issues. The pre-publication copy has these words on the cover: "Our planet faces a catastrophe if we do not satisfy the growing thirst of its people and the agriculture that sustains them. . . . The situation is critical and needs immediate action." In March, 1999, Travis Engen, the chief executive officer of ITT, wrote a guest editorial for the *Financial Times* of London in which he said, "It is time for the world's political, scientific and business leaders not only to take notice of this pending catastrophe, but to stand up and take action." In Trinidad the largest desalination plant in this hemisphere is being built with a U.S. firm, Ionics, involved. In Tampa, Florida, the largest desalination plant in the U.S. is under construction and local authorities are planning a second plant. The cost of producing desalinated water is gradually coming down, while the cost of fresh water is rising.

Meanwhile, an increasing number of small journals are recognizing the problem. *Industry Week* ran a story that reported, "The world may be running out of fresh water, and manufacturers are feeling parched." *Technocracy Digest* carried a story under the simple but blunt headline: "Water Wars Are Coming." Almost anything that calls attention to the problem is helpful. Water reuse is growing, but slowly, much too slowly. Unfortunately, interest by U.S. public officials is limited. Senator Harry Reid of Nevada has provided some leadership while others, including Senator Carl Levin of Michigan and Representative Jan Schakowsky of Illinois, have expressed interest. But until the subject becomes "hot," interest will be limited. By the time it heats up it may be too late to avoid serious harm to much of humanity.

An exception to the disinterest is the Middle East. As I write this, the movement toward peace has hit a sizable bump in the road. But I sense that events will force leaders on both sides to renew their efforts, however awkwardly it happens. Water is being discussed in the negotiations that have taken place. This book has been translated into Arabic and far more Middle Eastern leaders know about its content than do American leaders because the problem is a pressing one there. A few weeks ago I went to Syria and Jordan to meet with leaders there and to urge them toward a regional approach to their water problems, working with the Israelis and the Palestininans. Because of the tensions in that area, progress may be slow, but they know the time bomb of water is ticking. In Amman, the capital of Jordan, people can turn on the water in their homes one day a week; Jordan's population will grow by one-third in the next ten years.

There is an emerging consensus in Israel and her Arab neighbors that the long-run answer will be desalination, but it is already too late to provide the water from that source for the needs that will press that area in the immediate future. Constructing a desalination plant does not happen overnight, and the area will need many of them. Interim relief is being explored, with transporting water from Turkey by ship and huge plastic bubbles on the agenda as this is being written. Assisting in the brainstorming is the Washington-based Center for Middle East Peace and Cooperation headed by former Congressman Wayne Owens. As a people and as a government, the United States is generally effective in reacting to crises.

However, on this issue we must anticipate the crises and prevent them from occurring. That will take enlightened leadership, which I hope will emerge from those who read this book. Another part of this problem where the United States could play a key role in leadership is to urge the United Nations or the World Bank to create a body of international technicians who can monitor water agreements. The reality is that in the Middle East—and I can easily cite other regional examples—Jordanian technicians do not trust Israeli technicians, and vice versa. Syrian technicians do not trust Turkish technicians, and the Turks do not trust the Syrians. Reaching difficult regional agreements is an important part of the battle, but those agreements can evolve into gunfire unless a monitoring mechanism that both sides can trust is created.

There *are* answers to the problems we will confront, but there are no quick ones.

—Paul Simon
November, 2001

PREFACE

Every author believes his or her book is important. But this book has the potential to do more good for humanity than any manuscript I have written.

The significance of water problems gradually grew on me as I dealt with difficulties around the world as a member of the Senate Foreign Relations Committee. The realities gradually overwhelmed me, and I came to realize that the message of what is happening and will happen has to be delivered to this nation and the world. I hope this book will play a role in that.

I am grateful to many people who have helped in its production. They include my wife Jeanne, my brother Art, and (listed alphabetically) Leon Awerbuch, Jeletta Brant, John Briscoe, Ben Dziegielewski, Eric Edwards, Werner Fornos, Christopher Lant, Mike Lawrence, Gordon Leitner, Thomas McDermott, Mike Personnett, Senator Harry Reid, Joyce Starr, Catherine Van Heuven, Judy Wagner, and Larry Werner. Before his untimely death, Dr. Kurt Stehling provided valuable insights.

All of them have contributed to the end product, but the views expressed are mine and do not necessarily reflect those of these generous people. My former secretary in Washington, Jackie Williams, typed the rough drafts of the first chapters and then when

I moved from Washington Marilyn Lingle completed the task of plowing through my notes and typing. Steve Zidek chased down some of the detailed information in the book.

I thank all of them, as well as you who read these words, who have bestirred yourselves enough to get the book, and I hope do something after reading it.

PAUL SIMON
Southern Illinois University
Carbondale, Illinois

SECTION ONE

THE PROBLEM

1

AN OVERVIEW:
WORLD POPULATION AND WATER

By the gift of water You nourish and sustain us and all living things." These are the words used in the baptismal rite in Lutheran services.[1] But in our world increasing numbers of people cannot assume they will be nourished and sustained, and within a few years, a water crisis of catastrophic proportions will explode on us—unless aroused citizens in this and other nations demand of their leadership actions reflecting vision, understanding, and courage. Political leadership on water issues—as in every other field—tends to be shortsighted. But on water, shortsightedness could be cataclysmic. It is no exaggeration to say that the conflict between humanity's growing thirst and the projected supply of usable, potable water will result in the most devastating natural disaster since history has been accurately recorded, unless something happens to stop it.

The world's population of 5.9 billion will double in the next forty to ninety years, depending on whose estimates you accept. Our water supply, however, is constant. Compounding those grim realities is the fact that per capita world water consumption is rising twice as fast as the world's population. You do not have to be an Einstein to understand that we are headed toward a potential calamity.

Nations fight over oil, but valuable as it is, there are substitutes for oil. There is no substitute for water. We die quickly without water, and no nation's leaders would hesitate to battle for adequate water supplies. A decade ago U.S. intelligence services identified ten potential flashpoints where war could break out over water. I no longer have access to that type of information since leaving the Senate, but I know the number is higher today and will be much higher a decade from now. At least 300 million people live in regions of severe water shortages. By the year 2025, it will be three billion. A child born in 1960 in the Middle East or North Africa entered a region where the fresh water available annually was 3,430 cubic meters per capita. By the time that person reaches the age of 65, in the year 2025, it will be 667 cubic meters a year per capita, a drop of approximately 80 percent. Anywhere on our globe there are statistics nearly as dramatic. With three-quarters of the earth's surface covered by water, it may be hard to believe we can be headed toward a crisis based on water deficiencies, but 97 percent of that resource is saltwater, and perhaps two-thirds of the remainder consists of icebergs and snow.

Although we are nearing a crisis, concern by the public and political leaders is just beginning to emerge.

I have a long-standing interest in the problems of world hunger and the related hazard of excessive global population growth. When I served in the U.S. House of Representatives, I chaired an informal, bipartisan group of members who met regularly on these issues. I wrote two books on world hunger, one co-authored with my brother, Arthur Simon, who became the founding president of Bread for the World, the nation's largest citizens' lobby on hunger. In those books, we barely mentioned the water issue because it did not loom large on the earth's horizon. As late as 1982, an excellent book, *The Causes of World Hunger*, edited by Father William Byron, S.J., gives only passing mention to water. Five years later, the World Commission on Environment and Development, chaired by Norway's fine former prime minister Gro Harlem Brundtland, issued a 383-page report, devoting only one-half page to water.

A few magazines publish hints about the severe difficulties ahead. You may find a small circle of knowledgeable people discussing it, but it would be conservative to estimate that 10,000 times more media attention was devoted to the recent O.J. Simpson trials than to the approaching water crisis. But here and there are small signals. The international organization of the Rotary Clubs held a conference in the Netherlands in 1991 on the topic "Water: Tomorrow's Crucial Resource." In 1993 *National Geographic*, for only the second time in its 105-year-old history, had a special edition, titled simply "Water." In his introductory explanation for this extraordinary special edition, editor William Graves noted: "The problem is simply people—our increasing numbers and our flagrant abuse of one of our most precious, and limited, resources."[2] In his 1995 annual *State of the World*, Worldwatch Institute's Lester Brown reported: "Concern over water scarcity is rising."[3] The *Financial Mail* of South Africa commented in September 1995: "The most frightening of the many statistics for the future [of] South Africa are those related to water."[4] A bulletin of the International Food Policy Research Institute begins with these words: "Reform of water policy is urgently needed."[5] The heading of the bulletin: "Dealing With Water Scarcity in the Next Century." *Time* magazine reports: "At the moment, countries are poised to go to war over oil, but in the near future, water could be the catalyst for armed conflict."[6] Dr. Wally N'Dow, whom the *Los Angeles Times* describes as "the world's foremost specialist on cities," says bluntly: "In the past fifty years nations have gone to war over oil. In the next fifty we are going to go to war over water. The crisis point is going to be fifteen to twenty years from now."[7] But voices like these are isolated and largely ignored.

Buried in all the daily news trivia, the careful reader can find strong warnings about our future. The *Financial Times* of London begins a story: "Water, like energy in the late 1970s, will probably become the most critical natural resource issue facing most parts of the world by the start of the next century."[8] The British publication, *People and the Planet*, predicts that by the year 2025 at least sixty-five nations will experience serious water shortages.[9] Another British journal, *Worldlink*, the magazine of the World Economic Forum, has a cover article titled "Water: The Next Source of Trouble."[10] A scholarly journal on international law calls the shortage of fresh water "the national security issue of the twenty-first century."[11] "Water Crisis Looms, World Bank Says" is the heading of a story on an inside page of the *Washington Post* of August 3, 1995. The Associated Press story accompanying that heading quotes World Bank Vice President for Environmentally Sustainable Development Ismail Serageldin: "We are warning the world that there is a huge problem looming out there. . . . The experts all agree on the need to do something fast. The main problem is the lack of political will to carry out these recommendations."

That is the crux of the matter: political will. That is not going to be generated by World Bank reports. It must come from aroused citizens who understand the severity of the problem and demand action. Almost four centuries ago, a British writer noted: "Water is a very good servant, but it is a cruel master."[12]

"If you want to save your children from poverty, pay attention to water," Shimon Peres, then Israel's foreign minister, told a 1994 National Press Club forum in Washington.[13] Middle Eastern leaders who are usually reluctant to agree on anything are unanimous in saying that severe water shortages lie ahead in that region, and unless this difficulty is solved, armed confrontation is almost inevitable. Lack of water can have profound economic and military consequences.

There is a touch of prophecy in the old saying that harkens back to the era of the Wild West: "Whiskey is for drinking, and water is for fighting over." A national leader *may* take his nation to war over the threat of the loss of oil, but no leader can tolerate the loss of water without a belligerent response. If it takes years of negotiations for California and Nevada to agree on the allocation of the Truckee River waters, it should not come as a surprise that it took nine years to get hostile neighbors India and Pakistan to agree on the Indus River basin, and that India, Pakistan, and Bangladesh have been negotiating since 1960 on the Ganges River basin.* The complicated Danube River basin agreement in Europe is supervised by a task force of twelve nations, seven international organizations, and four nongovernmental groups.

Everyone can agree with U.S. Supreme Court Justice Oliver Wendell Holmes that "a river is more than an amenity, it is a trea-

---

*A river basin is the geographical area in which the streams and rivers flow into a large river.

7

sure."[14] There are more than 200 river basins in the world that are shared by at least two countries and over 2,000 treaties on these shared resources. The first water treaty, signed by two nations using the Weser River in Europe, goes back to the year 1221. Even when nations are on the best of terms, like Canada and the United States, there are serious disagreements on water-sharing issues. Our two countries manage our problems without resorting to arms, but who can say what will happen in the Middle East where there are no water surpluses and where the relationships between countries have a stormy history. By the year 2020, the most conservative estimate is that thirty-five nations will have severe water scarcity problems. Their leaders will not simply issue press statements. More than a dozen nations receive most of their water from rivers that cross borders of neighboring countries viewed as hostile. The word *rival* comes from Latin, meaning "someone who shares the same stream." Those who want a world of peace not only must look at stopping nuclear tests and reducing the arms race, but also at the troublesome issue of water.

In the 1962 book *Silent Spring*, which stirred the nation, Rachel Carson wrote: "In an age when man has forgotten his origins and is blind even to his most essential needs for survival, water along with other resources has become the victim of his indifference."[15] When she wrote that, water *quantity* problems were only a tiny dark cloud on the horizon.

One source notes: "Water is being withdrawn from [the world's] underground stores (aquifers) many times faster than it is being replaced by nature. . . . The rate of *net* withdrawal today is roughly equal to the flow of the Colorado River."[16] Similar illustrations are emerging around the globe almost unnoticed, like the silent start of a plague. It is only the beginning. No knowledgeable person disputes the conclusion of Pacific Institute founder and president Peter Gleick: "Fresh water is an increasingly precious resource."[17]

United Nations authorities underscore that with this simple statistic: 9,500 children a day die either because of lack of water or, more frequently, because of diseases caused by polluted water.[18] If one 747 plane filled with 350 children were to crash, killing all those on board, we would be mesmerized by the television and radio reports, and the story would fill the front pages of our newspapers. Yet at least sixteen times that many children die each day for water-related reasons, but they do it quietly, and their stories rarely reach our living room TV sets and seldom even appear in the back pages of our newspapers. In Africa, the world's fastest growing continent with a population of 750 million that is projected to double in twenty years, 40 percent of the population is expected to suffer serious illnesses over the next decade—frequently fatal—because of water-related problems.

A century ago, the leading killer of children in the United States was malaria. Today, it is almost nonexistent here. A variety of methods has been used to dramatically reduce the population of the mosquitoes that carry the disease. But around the world each year, 1 to 2 million people die of this highly preventable disease that is water-related, and approximately 280 million are infected. Water-related diarrheal diseases are even worse, killing about 4 million people a year, 3.2 million of them children. A simple treatment with oral rehydration salts (ORT), costing about twenty cents per treatment, could save almost all of these lives. In 1991 "almost 40 percent of the cases of diarrhea in children were treated with ORT, averting about one million unnecessary deaths."[19] Schistosomiasis, a disease carried by a water snail found in standing water where people work and play and use it for toilet purposes, kills 200,000 people a year and debilitates another 200 million. Millions more have been hit by "river blindness" and guinea worm disease, less life-threatening than they are debilitating. Recently, thanks to the leadership of former president Jimmy Carter and the Carter Center, the number of those stricken by these diseases has been reduced. Even though these and other water-related afflictions can be prevented and/or treated relatively inexpensively by U.S. methods, these problems are likely to worsen with the growing water shortage, as desperate people use more contaminated water. "Bad water is better than no water," they reason.

That choice is dictated by the human body, which is composed of more than 70 percent water. It takes less than a 1 percent deficiency in our body's water to make us thirsty. A 5 percent deficit causes a slight fever. An 8 percent shortage causes the glands to stop producing saliva and the skin to turn blue. A person cannot walk with a 10 percent deficiency, and a 12 percent deficiency brings on death.[20] There are more excruciating ways to die than from lack of water—but there are not many. A minimum annual water intake to sustain human life (including food production) is 7,500 gallons a year. These figures take on greater significance when combined with the fact that two-thirds of the world's population have to go out of their homes to fetch drinking water, and in most of the third world nations as much as one-third of the daily calorie intake is used by women and children—the main water carriers—for obtaining water.

Ironically, the areas of the world with the fastest growing populations are also the areas with already severe water problems, and the shortages will get much worse. North Africa, sub-Saharan Africa, Central Asia, Mexico, and the Middle East all have rapidly growing populations and rapidly depleting water supplies. *Congressional Quarterly Researcher* reports: "In the Middle East and throughout the world, water is increasingly becoming the central political issue—and a matter of survival for literally billions of people."[21] More and more, in all parts of the world, there is a squeeze between urban populations and farmers for limited quantities of water, and the larger number of people in cities are starting to prevail. Water specialist Sandra Postel writes: "No one has tallied the effect on future food production of the progressive shift of water from agriculture to cities, combined with the many forms of unsustainable water use."[22]

While water sufficiency problems are not nearly as severe in the United States as in most nations, three of the fastest-growing large states—California, Texas, and Florida—also feel the squeeze on water supplies and soon will face major difficulties. As of 1996, five of the ten fastest growing cities in the United States are in those three states. It is significant that all three states, like many parts of the globe with serious shortages, have at their doorsteps huge amounts of water that still are too expensive to modify for major consumption purposes: ocean water.

A World Resources Institute study comments: "If all the world's water fit into a bathtub, the portion of it that could be used sustainably in any given year would barely fill a tea-spoon."[23] That is an exaggeration, but it illustrates a truth.

Without a surge in desalination research, many in the world will be able to repeat the well-known lines from Samuel Taylor Coleridge's poem, "The Rime of the Ancient Mariner," with new meaning:

> Water, water everywhere
> And all the boards did shrink;
> Water, water everywhere
> Nor any drop to drink.[24]

.   .   .

Maintaining water *quality* in a world of shortages is also a problem. Travelers to many nations are routinely warned to avoid drinking the water, even in luxury hotels. Many of us have experienced the results of not following that advice. Seeing people bathe, wash their clothes, and drink, all from the same obviously polluted body of water, is a common sight in much of the world. At least 1.5 billion people—probably more—do not have access to a minimally adequate supply of safe water, and approximately 3 billion lack sanitation facilities, a problem that is tied to water quality. Even in the United States we have such problems. A study reports that one-fourth of the water people in West Virginia drink is unsafe. An August 1995 story in the *New York Times* begins:

> Tap water in the Corn Belt is dangerously contaminated with agricultural weed-killers, posing serious health risks, according to a study released today by the Environmental Working Group.
>
> Herbicides were found in the drinking water of almost all 29 cities and towns tested. At 18, the levels exceeded Federal safety standards.
>
> The worst violations were found in Danville, Illinois, where the level of the weed-killer cyanizine in one sample was 34 times the Federal standard. In Fort Wayne, Indiana, a single glass of water showed nine kinds of herbicides.[25]

The article suggests that the dangers are particularly severe for young children.

The United States is ahead of almost all nations in water quality, yet in one brief period bacteria in the water supply of Milwaukee caused more than 100 deaths and 4,400 to be hospitalized. But because we have worked over the decades to improve the quality of the water we use, our water is generally safer to drink than it once was, and our streams and lakes are cleaner. I can remember when there were no fish in the Illinois River, and now as I travel through my state, I see people fishing on the banks of the river or in boats, and I wonder how many of them know that government policy made this possible. The United States has doubled the numbers of lakes and rivers and streams in which people can fish and swim without danger. But the United States is not typical. However, the greater problem for the future of the world is not *quality* but *quantity*.

The World Bank estimates that eighty nations have water shortages severe enough to retard agricultural production. In almost all nations, including the United States, below-ground water tables, called aquifers, which are the source of much of the supply, are dropping, in some cases rapidly, and in a few areas this resource is depleted. With reduced per capita water availability almost inevitably comes reduced food availability. In less developed nations, as a whole, 90 percent of water use is for irrigation, and as the irrigation canals dry up, food production declines.

It is hard for many to understand the dimensions of the problem, including farmers who all of their lives have been accustomed to ample water supplies for irrigation.

I wish those who are skeptical about water warnings could have joined Senator Harry Reid of Nevada and me on a trip to Uzbekistan. We visited what had been a port city on the Aral Sea, once the third largest inland sea in the world. Some years prior to that, Soviet engineers convinced Nikita Khrushchev and other leaders that they could, for irrigation purposes, divert water that flowed into the Aral Sea, particularly to increase cotton production (an old dream of Lenin). They gave assurances that while there might be a temporary decline in water to the Aral Sea, soon the runoff would replenish the sea, and no harm would result.

Senator Reid and I stood at the edge of what had been a harbor and looked down perhaps seventy-five feet to dry land. It was dry much farther than we could see, dry for approximately the next fifty miles. The formerly huge runoff from the Amu Darya and Syr Darya Rivers had dropped to nothing. The fishing industry in the Aral Sea in the 1950s supported 60,000 jobs; now, none. Two-thirds of the Aral Sea's water has disappeared, and agricultural lands around the sea have reduced production because of greater salinity, the salt blown by the winds from the now dry land. A World Bank report has this cryptic epitaph for the Aral Sea: "Costs for full restoration of this hypersaline dead water body are prohibitive."[26] Thirty million people have been adversely affected.

Senator Reid and I visited a clinic run by U.S. volunteers dealing with unexpected health problems, particularly lung difficulties that arose because of dry salt and toxic dust in the air. According to a 1989 study, two-thirds of the people in the area surrounding the Aral Sea are suffering "from hepatitis, typhoid, gastrointestinal diseases, or throat cancer. Especially affected are the children, who suffer from . . . anemia, rickets and liver complaints."[27] In 1997 a local physician told the *New York Times* much the same story: "We are seeing a very high incidence of anemia, especially among children. Cancers have increased. Stomach and intestinal diseases are very common. People's kidneys and livers cannot stay healthy in an environment like this."[28] Infant mortality rates are four times that of the rest of the former Soviet Union. Soviet leaders told the Aral Sea ship captains that the water would return, and in the old Soviet Union, when the government told you not to move a ship, you did not move your ship. There, in this "harbor," were hulks of large boats marooned fifty miles from water.

In less dramatic ways, the Aral Sea disaster is happening on every continent. Water specialist Sandra Postel writes about this in a magazine article titled "Where Have All the Rivers Gone?"[29] She describes the gradual shrinkage of three American rivers, as well as those in other nations. One is the Colorado River, which drains 244,000 square miles—an area larger than France, though in volume of flow it is only sixth among U.S. rivers. It provides water to seven states. The Colorado watershed includes 2 million acres of farmland and 21 million people and is the most rapidly growing population area in the United States.

In China I met with university officials about that nation's water difficulties. China's already serious problems are going to become infinitely more serious. In a nation with huge food demands and half of its cropland under irrigation, China may have to significantly reduce irrigation. China's Minister of Water Resources observes: "In rural areas, over 81 million people find it difficult to procure water. In urban areas, the shortages are even worse. More than 300 Chinese cities are short of water and 100 of them are very short."[30] China has 22 percent of the world's population but only 7 percent of the world's cropland and 7 percent of the world's freshwater. Qu Geping, head of China's Environmental Protection Agency, says that the ideal population for China's water supply is 650 million, but today the nation has almost twice that number, and the population is still climbing.

In the past twenty-one years, the international demand for water has doubled, and unless there are herculean efforts at conservation and research, less dramatic and more tragic scenes than the Aral Sea will unfold: dry dirt, dust, and desert where productive fields now exist, and with that will come food shortages that cause reduction in average life span and misery for much of the world. Many lakes and wetland areas will disappear, and of those that survive, sizable numbers will have increased salt content, diminishing their ability to provide assistance in growing food.

There are ways to avoid the looming waterless storm. The later chapters of this book spell out the answers. However, we are inching toward solutions when the grim realities require us to take giant strides. Unless the environmental movement, leaders of our religious communities, and others with a sense of responsibility for the future mobilize and mount a substantial effort to alter the present course, the years ahead will not provide either a brighter civilization or one that we would recognize today. Expect average life spans to drop dramatically, and wars to multiply.

The most disturbing scenes of human suffering I have ever viewed were in Somalia, before U.S. troops went in to relieve the situation. Hundreds of thousands starved to death. Starvation from lack of food is a slow process. Human beings can live several weeks without food, and while shortage of water is often the cause of the lack of food (complicated in Somalia by the almost total lack of government), people can live only a few days without water. The massive numbers dying for lack of both food and water will be seen by all of us over and over and over again if the world does not act, and action requires U.S. leadership. No other nation has our capability and resources to lead.

The question is whether we will.

2

CALIFORNIA

The award-winning movie *Chinatown*, starring Jack Nicholson and Faye Dunaway, centers on a murder committed in a struggle over California water rights. That 1974 film could become more prophetic than the producers imagined.

California has a population of 31 million—more people than Canada and 161 other nations—and despite earthquakes and floods, it is growing at a rate of 2.7 percent annually, a greater growth than most nations experience. In less than thirty years, California's 31 million people will be 48 to 60 million, depending upon whose forecast is correct. What will these figures mean for future water use in California? After a yearlong study, a 119-page 1995 report concluded:

California's current water use is unsustainable. In many areas, ground water is being used at a rate that exceeds the rate of natural replenishment. This is causing land to subside and threatening some aquifers with possible collapse. The use of ground water is almost entirely unmonitored and uncontrolled. . . . Urban water use is inefficient and poorly managed. Agricultural policies encourage the production of water-intensive, low-valued crops. . . . Fish and wildlife species are being destroyed by withdrawal of water, as well as by development. . . . Official projections are that water demand will exceed available supplies [in the year 2020] by several million acre feet—a gap projected in every official "California Water Plan" produced since 1957.[1]

That is not heartening news from the nation's most populous state, and one with more than 1,400 large water reservoirs and the most sophisticated water supply system in the world. Even in the relatively water-rich northern part of the state, guests at the San Francisco Marriott (and probably other hotels) are greeted by a small sign in the bathroom:

PLEASE HELP US CONSERVE
OUR MOST VALUABLE RESOURCE, WATER.

Because we are all interdependent, when officials tell California's farmers to use substantially less water—as they did in 1992—the prices of fruits and vegetables rise in Illinois and other parts of the nation. Few, if any, consumers in New Jersey or Indiana pick up fruit, notice a higher price, and say to themselves, "Prices must be higher because California had to cut back on irrigation." Half of all vegetables and fruits consumed in the United States come from California. That state is heavily dependent on the shrinking Colorado River, and on melting snows that are not increasing. Southern California receives on average less than ten inches of rain annually, while Chicago has thirty-three inches and New York City, forty-four inches. People are generally aware that there is more rain in the eastern United States than in most of our western states but do not understand the almost total dependence of California and some other states on the transportation of water to sustain life. Here is one author's description of three California cities: "Inhabited California, most of it, is by strict definition a semidesert. Los Angeles is drier than Beirut; Sacramento as dry as the Sahel; San Francisco is only half as wet as Mexico City. . . . There was not a single tree growing in San Francisco when the first Spanish arrived."[2] The Metropolitan Water District of Southern California, serving 16 million people, estimates that the existing water supply will meet only 43 percent of the demand for the district in the year 2010. The district imports a majority of its water either from the Colorado River or pipes it from the northern part of the state. But a 1995 report from their chief engineer notes: "Reliability of future imported water supplies is decreasing. . . . Recent evidence indicates that reductions in water supply reliability will discourage plant and equipment investment in the state, which will translate directly into lost production, reductions in income, and lost jobs."[3]

Inevitably there will be more stories like the one under the heading in the *Los Angeles Times* about the new campus for the University of California: "UC Selects Merced Campus," and the subhead reads: "The Availability of Water Is the Deciding Factor."[4] San Diego mayor Susan Golding says, "Water Is the basis of economics here."[5] At least one California city had its bond rating lowered by Standard and Poor's because of water shortages, and more will follow. And those are extremely minor problems, compared to the serious crises California and other states—and many nations—will confront in a few years. If California's leaders do not exercise prudence and wisdom, and if they fail to show any long-term vision, the southern part of the state will see dry wells, water tables that disappear or are dangerously lower with substantial saltwater seepage, home use of water dramatically reduced, lawns and gardens that cannot be watered, and industries that will dry up and blow away like much of the farmland. The "dust bowl" experience of the 1930s that brought "Okies" to California from parched Oklahoma and other states could be repeated in reverse, scattering significant portions of the Pacific Coast state's population.

A 1957 California water plan predicted that the state would eventually have 19.7 million acres of irrigated land, but it reached its peak fourteen years later at 9.5 million acres, and the combination of urban growth and salinated soil forced the number to gradually decline.

But California has at least studied its problems. Most states and most nations have not looked at what the coming decades will bring in water supply difficulties. The Pacific Institute report on California is the most comprehensive look at any state's water situation.

Those who prepared it encountered difficulties. They discovered: "No one knows for sure how much ground water is used, by whom, and for what. . . . Residential, commercial, industrial, and municipal data on water use are spotty, at best. . . . On-farm water use is rarely measured directly."[6] If a sophisticated and wealthy state like California has inadequate data, it is understandable that less affluent states and third world countries have much less data. We know enough about water use and supply to realize that this nation and the world will face extreme problems. But adequately dealing with the coming crisis will require gathering much more data.

In some ways California mirrors the problem in much of the world. That is true for the nature of the water crisis, its growing severity, and for the answers. Like most of the world, California has water in abundance where people are not in abundance. Three-fourths of its snow and rain fall in the northern part of the state, where one-third of the people live. One-fourth of the precipitation is in the southern part of the state, where two-thirds of its citizens reside. Israel, as an international example, like California, has the bulk of its water resources in the north but its major water needs are in the south.

Early in this century, Los Angeles–area water authorities understood that they would face problems, so they purchased the third-largest body of water in the state, Owens Lake, and the property around the lake. It is 180 miles north and inland from Los Angeles. Today it is called Owens Dry Lake, because Los Angeles has sucked it dry. But the story does not end there. Like the Aral Sea in eastern Europe, when the wind blows on a dry day, particulate matter is sent into the air to the point that in some areas it is twenty times as high as the maximum safety standards for air pollution. Approximately twenty-five times a year the air in the region violates federal air quality standards. The U.S. Enviromental Protection Agency rates this area the worst in the nation, six times worse than the second-place polluter, the area surrounding the steel mills of Gary, Indiana.[7] The regional manager for air pollution says that sometimes as much as 4 million tons of fine, salty grit travels fifty miles or more. People in the area want Los Angeles to fill the lake again, but Los Angeles officials say that would require 10 percent of their water, something they cannot afford.[8]

Southern California is dependent on the Colorado River for half of its water, the present supply secured through an interstate compact negotiated over a lengthy period of time.[9] Even that is subject to change. A publication on water for the area notes: "Southern California has yet to feel the pinch of a 1964 U.S. Supreme Court decree holding that, in order to honor Arizona's entitlement, about 55 percent of [Southern California's] Colorado River allotment no longer would be available on a dependable basis."[10] Consider Marc Reisner's description of the Colorado River in his excellent book on the west, *Cadillac Desert*: "It is one of the siltiest rivers in the world . . . and one of the wildest. Its drop of nearly thirteen thousand feet is unequaled in North America. . . . It is the most legislated, most debated, and most litigated river in the entire world. . . . The river system provides over half the water of greater Los Angeles, San Diego and Phoenix. . . . It illuminates the neon city of Las Vegas, whose annual income is one-fourth the entire gross national product of Egypt—the only other place on earth where so many people are so helplessly dependent on one river's flow. The greater portion of the Nile, however, still manages . . . to reach its delta at the Mediterranean Sea. The Colorado is so used up on its way to the sea that only a bubbling trickle reaches its dried-up delta at the head of the Gulf of California, and then only in wet years."[11]

As is the case in much of the world, 80 percent of California's water goes for agricultural purposes, with its farmers not paying the full cost of receiving it. Similar to other areas, aquifers are being depleted. The two states with the highest levels of water withdrawal from aquifers and surface water are California and Idaho.

If there were such a thing as a water misery index, California would not be high on it today, but its rise on the index will be meteoric.

Unless.

Unless political leaders make sensible but painful decisions and make them soon. The major decisions needed are spelled out in uncomfortable detail later in this book.

3

LAS VEGAS

If the California forecast is grim because of water crises in its future, the Nevada forecast is grimmer.

Almost 70 percent of Nevadans live in the Las Vegas area. Clark County—home of Las Vegas—grew faster between 1990 and 1994 than any U.S. county with a population of over 500,000, a growth of 27 percent, bringing its population to 938,000. The 1997 population estimate is 1.2 million—a growth rate of more than 1,500 residents a week. Journalist Ernie Pyle gives you an idea of Nevada in 1930: "There was just one telephone book for the whole state! Every phone in Nevada was listed in it, plus four counties of adjoining California. And the whole thing made a thin little volume that you could stick in your topcoat pocket."[1] In 1920 Clark County had a population of 4,859, and a 1992 projection for the year 2030, 1,807,805,[2] has now changed to well over 2 million, some say more than 3 million. How long it can sustain its growing—or even its current—population is a serious question. The general manager of the Southern Nevada Water Authority warned that without a new supply of water, that area will have to stop all growth by the year 2000.[3] With new supplies of water from other parts of the state and Lake Mead, that forecast has been lengthened to 2006 or 2010.

After a visit to Las Vegas, one journalist summed up the situation with these nine words: "This booming desert city is running out of water."[4] But optimistic Nevadans recall the 1891 prophecy of a California business leader, later a prominent Nevada congressman: "Nevada is a dying state."[5]

Nevada is the most arid of our fifty states. In the summer of 1996, some communities in the Chicago area in a few hours suffered a cloudburst of twenty-four inches of rain—as much as Las Vegas normally receives in six years. Las Vegas, which will soon be bigger than Detroit, receives only four inches of rain a year. Las Vegas, like Southern California, is heavily dependent on the Colorado River for water. It is one of the longest rivers in the nation, but only sixth in terms of volume—one-twelfth the water volume of the Columbia River and one-twenty-sixth of the Mississippi. Its importance lies in the water-starved areas through which it rolls. In one of the most carefully researched studies on the legal and supply problems of the Colorado, the *Arizona State Law Journal* concluded: "The one thing that probably almost all parties interested in the Colorado River agree upon is that the existing Law of the River will not be adequate to meet the challenges of the twenty-first century."[6] The laws will be inadequate because the supply will be inadequate.

Las Vegas is solving its pressing shortage temporarily by piping water through the mountains from nearby areas of the state, bringing more water from Lake Mead, which helps sustain the city. But that gives Las Vegas only short-term relief. The *Engineering News-Record* reports that Las Vegas "may spend nearly $2 billion to pipe groundwater from as far as three hundred miles away"— and then still face a crisis.[7] Environmental author Philip Fradkin writes: "Nevada [had] the smallest population and service area, [and] the least amount of water when [the Colorado River] was apportioned between the seven states in 1922. Then something occurred that had not been foreseen; the region grew and grew and grew. . . . Nevada may be the first state in the Colorado River Basin to run out of water."[8] He also noted the conspicuous waste of water in Las Vegas, with casinos having cascading waterfalls and lavish fountains—two times the per capita national average consumption and three times that of Los Angeles. Then he added: "Much of the contemporary culture of the American Southwest is based on denying its desertness. . . . In a subdivision being built to the south [of Las Vegas], Paseo Verde Parkway and Val Verde Road intersect in Green Valley Ranch. The concept of green, like sod lawns, was an imported fantasy."

Conservationist Tom Jensen projects this future for Nevada and the Colorado River: "Imagine Lake Powell empty, plumes of wind-blown silt laced with salts and heavy metals lofted far across the Colorado Plateau from dry, exposed deltas. Imagine Lake Mead half-full, its hydroelectric turbines idle. Imagine the Colorado River reduced to a trickle, and that trickle reduced to a salty brine. Why imagine these things? Because the images represent a probable future for the Colorado River."[9]

Will Rogers once observed: "In the old days, ranchers shot each other over water. Today, it's a lot tougher: bureaucrats are in charge."[10] Complex decisions have to be made by leaders of government, with a huge impact on the lives of people within their jurisdictions. And in water-short regions, a transaction as simple as the sale of property from one party to another has to be treated differently than the sale of property in Illinois or New York. The Nevada Attorney General's office recommends: "To avoid title problems in any real property transaction, buyers and sellers should state explicitly what water rights, if any, they intend to transfer in the conveyance."[11] In the eastern part of the nation, if a river or stream cuts through property, the owner has a right to a portion of it, what are called "reasonable-use, riparian water rights." But in Nevada and Colorado and much of the west, land and water rights do not automatically go together and often require separate deeds. It is similar to mineral rights in the eastern part of the nation. A resident of Illinois can buy property but not own the subsurface rights to the oil or coal or natural gas that may be discovered on that real estate. In the West, there are people who identify themselves as water lawyers who advise individuals, corporations, and municipalities on the lease or purchase of water rights.

Nevada's water problem is not simply the insular difficulty of one state, even though its concerns are more pressing than those of any other state. Like most western states, Nevada is engaged in a struggle with its neighbors; it is also involved in the fight between its urban users, who are growing in number, and its farmers, who have traditionally been the chief beneficiaries of water projects.

The battle between the states is an old one that preceded statehood. In many areas of the West, water has always been a precious commodity, and human beings tend to fight over precious commodities, whatever their name, unless clear agreements are in place to avoid conflict.

Seven states—Arizona, California, Colorado, Nevada, New

Mexico, Utah, and Wyoming—signed an agreement in 1922, after decades of squabbling, that still governs state allocations of the Colorado River. When Congress approved the Colorado River Compact, it became the first agreement of this type between states that was ratified by the federal government. The compact divides the states into the upper basin (Colorado, New Mexico, Utah, and Wyoming) and the lower basin composed of the remaining states: Arizona, California, and Nevada. The upper and lower divisions each received an allocation of 7.5 million acre-feet of water per year. An acre-foot is the equivalent of an acre of water one foot deep, or 326,000 gallons. States in the upper part of the basin claim that, because of factors such as evaporation, they have only 6 million acre-feet available, rather than their allotted 7.5 million, but they now use only 4 million acre-feet. The allocations in the upper part of the basin do not present serious problems *yet*. The allocations in the lower division, which made sense in 1922, were 4.4 million acre-feet for California, 2.8 million for Arizona, and only 300,000 for Nevada, with its tiny population then of 71,000. The lower division projection for 1997 is that Arizona will use 2.25 million acre-feet, from an allotted 2.8 million; Nevada will use 240,000, from an allotted 300,000; and California will use 5.12 million, more than its allotted 4.4 million. That totals 7.61 million acre-feet, more than the agreement's 7.5 million. Complicating things further are Indian tribal claims approved by a 1908 U.S. Supreme Court decision and a 1944 agreement between the U.S. and Mexico to provide our southern neighbor 1.5 million acre-feet. A 1964 Supreme Court decree has the practical effect of allocating 917,000 acre-feet to five Indian tribes—more than three times the amount Nevada is permitted to receive.[12] Ten tribes in all hold rights along the river.

No one questions that the Colorado River is significantly

over-allocated. It provides water for 20 million people and irrigates more than 1 million acres. The river once flowed plentifully with fresh water into the sea. Now, when it reaches the ocean—and it does not always get there—it is loaded with salt and pesticides.

The 1964 Supreme Court decision, *Arizona v. California*, permits any lower-division Colorado River state the rights to the unused portion of another lower-division state. That makes it possible for California to use what Arizona and Nevada do not use. But Nevada knows it is headed for trouble and is "banking" some of its unused water at Lake Mead, and that banking will increase. Arizona, in the meantime, plans to put a banking operation into effect soon because that state's leaders also envision long-term problems. But if Nevada and Arizona use all their allotments, California will face an immediate crisis.

Article 9 of the Colorado River Compact, approved by Herbert Hoover while Secretary of Commerce, calls for court enforcement of the agreement. The agreement cannot be terminated except by unanimous agreement of all the states, which never will happen.

The political delicacy of this is illustrated by action that some Nevada and California officials took in 1995 and 1996 that appeared to make sense for both states. The Metropolitan Water District of Southern California entered into an agreement with the State of Nevada that called for Nevada to pay $53 million toward replacing an earthen irrigation canal in the Imperial Valley in California with a concrete one.[13] In exchange, the Metropolitan Water District would give Las Vegas 30,000 acre-feet of water a year. The California water officials believed that the concrete replacement of the canal would save more than 67,000 acre-feet of water. While the entire arrangement appeared to be unprecedented—one state paying for a public works project in another—it made sense for both states. Secretary of the Interior Bruce Babbit, whose actions on western land and water matters have been both sensible and courageous, praised the arrangement, but that only added to the concerns about the proposal by those who view him as an ogre.

Governor Pete Wilson of California said that the Metropolitan Water District was "usurping the authority of the state."[14] Fearing the worst, small water districts, not part of the negotiations, complained. California state senator Dave Kelley said, "The people I am talking to up and down the state are pretty upset about it."[15] Governor Fife Symington of Arizona threatened to go into court to stop the agreement, even though it did not diminish Arizona's allocation by one gallon.

The deal fell apart.

The *Arizona Republic* of Phoenix editorialized:

> Arizona ought to have in place a responsible plan to use its full entitlement of Colorado River water. . . . The unused portion is being eyed covetously as a possible permanent new source by the thirsty states of California and Nevada. . . . The creation of a water bank would have another salutary effect. The message it would send to California and Nevada would be unambiguous and forceful: Keep your hands off because the 2.8 million acre-feet per year is legally ours. . . . The only legitimate question is this: How soon can authorizing legislation be passed? To squander this opportunity would be tantamount to cutting our throats.[16]

Former Arizona governor Sam Goddard summed up the feeling of many Arizonans: "We've got to prepare for the ultimate and inevitable shortage. Arizona is a growing state. There's no way we can avoid it. People are coming. They'll be here. And the water we have from the Colorado River is the only way we're going to be able to sustain them."[17] Adding some substance to his concern is the growth of Phoenix from 30,000 people in 1922, when the Colorado River Compact was signed, to an estimated 1.1 million in 1996. Tucson and the outlying areas around it use 200,000 acre-feet of groundwater annually but replenish their aquifer at only 50,000 acre-feet a year, and with declining aquifers comes the inevitable deterioration in water quality. In the fall of 1995, the late mayor Herb Drinkwater—that was his name—of Scottsdale, a wealthy Phoenix suburb of 155,000, announced that there would be no more building permits for houses for eighteen months because of the water shortage.

But Arizona's lack of cooperation with neighboring states brought a reaction from the Southern Nevada Water Authority general manager, Patricia Mulroy: "It seems to defy logic. Here we are in desperate need for what is but a fraction of what they have, and they're trying to use it just so we can't have it. That really is the bottom line."[18]

Water issues are important and emotional. No political leader wants to appear to be giving up water to another state. That is part of the reason for the regular court fights that erupt over the Colorado River Compact.

Clouding the situation is the legal doctrine of "prior appropriation." This holds that those who first use surface water rights have permanent access to them, as long as the water resources are put "to beneficial use." Some fear that if Arizona leases water rights to another state, this legal doctrine of prior appropriation might cause Arizona to lose the permanent rights to the water because the state is not using the water for its own beneficial use. The American Society of Civil Engineers developed a Model State Water Rights Code that would correct some of these flaws, and parts of it have been adopted by a few states.

Exchanges between Arizona and Nevada officials have been particularly sharp. Governor Symington irritated Nevada officials in 1995 by saying, "If Las Vegas is outstripping its water resources, then they should curtail their growth. . . . They don't have any conservation plan. They are truly profligate in their water use."[19] There is partial validity to his charge. Las Vegas does use a per capita average of 330 gallons a day, three times higher than San Diego, and more than the 228 gallons a day average in Phoenix. But much of that high per capita use is because of large numbers of tourists. Las Vegas limits the size of lawns, controls the hours in which they can be watered, and has other restrictions with penalties enforced by water police. Nevada officials counter Governor Symington's charges by noting that the huge multibillion-dollar Central Arizona Project that helps Arizona's water situation was built in part by Nevada taxpayers. They also argue that Arizona does not use all of its allocation from the Colorado River, and uses part of the water it gets for marginally profitable and water-intensive crops like hay and alfalfa. While Arizona has three times the population of Nevada, it has nine times as much water available. Phoenix and Tucson each get two to three times as much rainfall as Las Vegas. Both Arizona and Nevada officials do no harm to themselves politically by standing up vigorously for the water rights of their states, but the escalating charges and countercharges make resolving the issues more difficult. Half a century ago, John Gunther wrote about the state of Colorado what he could write today about many western states: "Water is blood in Colorado. Touch water, and you touch everything; about water the state is as sensitive as a carbuncle."[20]

Several creative ideas have surfaced to resolve Las Vegas's future difficulties, and most of them have been shot down. One of the more realistic proposals called for Nevada building a dam in Colorado on Roan Creek, and in exchange for doing that, a pipeline would supply water to Las Vegas. Colorado would benefit from the recreational advantages of the project, and Las Vegas would get the water. But after studying that proposal, Governor Roy Romer of Colorado rejected the idea.

David Hogan, a water expert with the Southwest Center for Biological Diversity, has this assessment: "I can't think of a less sustainable city in the West than Las Vegas. Las Vegas is just one large house of cards, ready to come down. Take away one resource card [water], and the rest will come tumbling down."[21]

·   ·   ·

What can be done to assure a water supply for Las Vegas's future? There are no simple, dramatic answers, but the pieces of the puzzle bear a similarity to those in other water-short areas. There are solid solutions, but whether we have the foresight and political courage to achieve those solutions is doubtful.

4

FLORIDA AND OTHER STATES

In some ways Florida's water problems are similar to California's: shortages, despite water at its doorstep; mushrooming population, a larger rate of growth than California, but in a much smaller body of land; problems with salinity of the soil and irrigation; and a desalination process in use, but in its infancy.

In 1950 Florida had a population of 2.77 million and lived comfortably with its water supplies. By 1990 the population had grown to 13 million and water quantity and quality problems surfaced. Florida's population will be 20 million by 2020—and even the most optimistic planners know that spells critical water difficulties.

Florida's conservation-insensitive cultural habits, involving activities as basic as garbage disposal, represent a great threat to the sea, the sea that must be used more and more by all humanity. And just as Florida represents a greater threat to the sea than California, the sea represents a greater long-term natural threat to Florida than it does to California.

Scientists are divided on whether there is a global warming trend, but a large majority believe that while there is variation from year to year, the overall trend is toward warming. (This is discussed more in Chapter 7.) With warming will come an increase in melting of snow, glaciers, and icebergs and a rise in the level of the ocean, greater than the normal rise and fall that usually takes place. If there is a significant rise in the ocean level, as a some scientists predict, the consequences for low-lying Florida could be devastating. This general truth applies to Florida: *Whatever causes addition to the sea, and lifts water levels, harms Florida; whatever consumes seawater and diminishes the likelihood of elevation, or lowers it, helps Florida.*

Paul and Anne Ehrlich are more pessimistic than most scientific observers, but they are thoughtful and responsible researchers and authors. Listen to their description of Florida:

> The state is low and flat; the bottom of Lake Okeechobee is at sea level. The 2- or 3-foot rise in sea level that may occur in the next half century [because of the earth's warming] would flood a substantial portion of the state. . . . The porous limestone shelf on which most of the state rests will permit salt to penetrate aquifers far inland as sea level rises. It has been estimated that for every foot of rise in sea level, there will be about a 40-foot reduction in the depth of freshwater in Florida aquifers. Indeed, the threat of salinization is already present because of human manipulation of surface water flows even without rising seas. . . . Climate change due to greenhouse warming also could greatly exacerbate Florida's freshwater supply problems.[1]

There are practical economic reasons why Floridians should be environmentalists! Referring to the climate trend and its significance on the sea level, Senator Albert Gore Jr., writing before he became vice-president, said: "According to some predictions . . . up to 60 percent of the present population of Florida may have to be relocated."[2] Most scientists, however, are not that pessimistic.

Even if these gloomy predictions turn out to be largely incorrect, and the sea rises only an inch or two, Florida will have problems. A hurricane that now affects mostly the coastal areas will move farther inland with a rising sea. Saltwater will invade more aquifers.

The United States is signatory to an effort to establish international air pollution standards that can diminish global warming, a problem that brings health threats, such as increased skin cancer because of the thinning of the ozone layer, as well as a rising ocean level. The aim is to establish binding agreements among the industrial nations by the year 2000, but that will not be easy. Automobile manufacturers in our country are worried that they will be harmed; China is heavily dependent on coal for energy and that government is wary; the list of countries and industries that might be temporarily harmed is a lengthy one, and that makes negotiations difficult. But Florida's concerns are by no means limited to the threat of a rising ocean.

A glance at newspaper headlines in Florida in the mid-1990s makes it clear that there are troubles looming: "Counties Set to War over Water," "Barricade the Water," "Shortage Could Dry up Economy," "Water Resources in Jeopardy," "Clock Is Ticking in Search for Water," "Battles Mount in Thirsty Florida," "West Coast [of Florida] Faces Future Water Woes," "Water Levels Down Despite Drop in Use." There are many more examples.

The shortage is not of headlines but of water. Florida developed a state water plan in 1995. The foreword to the plan summarizes the situation: "Florida's economic future and quality of life are tied to water resources. . . . In many areas of the state, the prospects for new . . . inexpensive, clean sources of water no longer exist."[3] The report notes that there are "both quality and quantity problems. Ninety percent of the state's population depends on groundwater, and the groundwater is highly susceptible to contamination from . . . municipal landfills, leaking underground storage tanks, hazardous waste dumps, septic tanks, and agricultural pesticides." Florida's aquifers are shallower than any other state's, making Florida more vulnerable to pollution than others. And the overpumping of aquifers that is taking place results in saltwater intrusion. That intrusion "is already a problem all up the west coast [of Florida]," U.S. Representative Karen Thurman told a 1995 panel.[4]

Mark Farrell, a Florida water official, summarizes their situation with these words: "Our environment is being seriously compromised by traditional ground and surface water withdrawals."[5] Marine biologist Sylvia Earle writes: "Sudden death came to Florida Bay in 1993. . . . It is difficult to pin down the precise cause or causes . . . but no one doubts that it is one of thousands of man-made disasters now sweeping the oceans. High concentrations of fertilizers, pesticides, herbicides, and other exotic chemicals flowing primarily from large agricultural developments in south Florida, especially sugar plantations, coupled with decades of diversion and manipulation of traditional sources of freshwater, are believed to be responsible for the wholesale collapse of the bay's ecosystem."[6] Another Florida official comments: "The chamber of horrors that everybody predicted [years ago] is coming true."[7]

The 1999 Florida water plan states that "demands for water are beginning to exceed the sustainable yield of aquifers and surface waters."[8] Throughout the study there are references to "increasingly threatened water resources." In central Pasco County, for example, many wells that were ten feet below the surface seven years ago are now twenty-eight feet below the surface. While Florida averages fifty-three inches of rainfall a year, thirty-eight inches of that evaporates into the atmosphere.

What is now only the sighting of a dark cloud in Florida freshwater problems will soon emerge as a much more serious threat. Florida does not yet have the water concerns that California and Nevada have, but before long Floridians will have serious difficulties, even if there is no rise in sea level. People at the top of Florida's government know this. Among other problems, Florida's source for most of its water is a series of shallow aquifers, aquifers that when drawn below a certain level have seepage from the sea that can make the water unfit for drinking, irrigation, or industrial purposes.

We think of wildlife and plant life when we read about Florida's 500,000-acre marsh, but that same swampland performs a huge unseen service for the state by recharging the aquifers. The replenishment is not as great as the withdrawal, but without the swamp, Florida's future water difficulties would be much more severe. And housing and urban sprawl developments compound the problems.

·   ·   ·

Having an adequate supply of water and knowing that its content is safe is something most of us assume as part of our daily lives. But this is not true for many Americans.

Florida, as well as California, Nevada, and others along the Colorado River, are not the only states to experience water difficulties. Without pretending to give a comprehensive state-by-state look at these problems, here are a few examples:

- Virginia and North Carolina have a "water war" over Lake Gaston, a body of water that lies within both states. To resolve water shortages in the Virginia Beach area, the state of Virginia planned a $240 million, 76-mile pipeline from the lake to the city, but North Carolina got a federal court injunction to stop construction of the pipeline until the Federal Energy Regulatory Commission could provide an environmental impact statement. Opponents argued that the pipeline "would seriously deplete the flow . . . which feeds the lake, threatening fish and endangering northeastern North Carolina's economic livelihood."[9] In mid-1997 the U.S. Court of Appeals for the District of Columbia ruled 2-1 that the withdrawal of water from Lake Gaston for Virginia Beach did not violate the Clean Water Act and that the Federal Energy Regulatory Commission acted within its mandate in authorizing the withdrawal.[10] North Carolina is fighting that decision with two separate appeals.

  Since water resources like Lake Gaston rarely follow conventional borders of countries, states, or municipalities, dealing with the apportionment of the use of water gets complicated. The *Norfolk Virginian-Pilot*'s description of Virginia Beach could aptly fit many cities soon: "The lack of a municipal water supply . . . has slowly been choking that state's largest city. Water restrictions, imposed three years ago, have left residents' lawns brown and cars dirty; the lack of water also has helped slow the city's growth to a trickle."[11] The irony of the situation is that Virginia Beach, as the name implies, is right on the ocean. A huge amount of water is at the city's doorstep, but the ability to use it is limited by current lack of emphasis on research into converting saltwater to freshwater. Wells provide some water to the area, but the wells near the ocean contain three to five times as much salt as most wells in the United States.

Virginia identifies thirty-two communities with poor water quality, including two with a population of more than 13,000.

- Montana, although technically a water-surplus state, has so many problems that it adopted a Management Dispute Resolution System. Montana's water quality has been worsening for years, causing a controversial referendum on water quality in the fall election of 1996. Two examples from the *Washington Post* make clear why there are strong emotions on this issue in Montana:

> Butte . . . once known as "the richest hill on Earth" when it was producing $25 billion worth of copper, is now a monstrous festering sore on the landscape. Butte's Berkeley Pit, closed as an open pit copper mine in 1982, is now filling up with a toxic cauldron of heavy-metal-laced water—28 billion gallons and still rising. The Clark Fork River is contaminated for nearly a hundred miles. . . .
>
> In north-central Montana . . . Zortman Mining Inc. agreed to a nearly $37 million settlement with the state and federal government over long-standing water quality violations.[12]

- Water-rich Oregon in 1990 adopted a Conservation and Efficient Water Use Plan that requires new applicants for municipal water to submit conservation plans. Irrigation districts that hope to have the conserved water also must present a plan to show careful use of this resource. A 1995 report of the U.S. Department of Agriculture lists seventy-eight Oregon rural communities with water quality problems, and twenty-seven with quantity problems.

- In the northern quarter of Pottawatomie County in Oklahoma, mentioned in one of literally hundreds of documents about rural America before me as I type this, there are 350 households without public water service, which suffer from both quality and quantity problems.

- Abbeville County, South Carolina, has 1,000 homes without running water. It is one of thirty-seven communities in South Carolina listed by the Department of Agriculture as having no running water.

- The same report lists 377 rural Kentucky communities with poor quality water.

- Even in relatively affluent Hawaii, there are more than 15,000 homes without running water.

- Less than 1 percent of the population of Pennsylvania lacks running water, but to "maintain and supply clean water" to all the residents of the state would take an estimated investment of $3.4 billion.

- Michigan has a plentiful supply of water, but when the Department of Agriculture announced in 1995 that more than thirty-five Michigan communities had quality problems, the agency heard from "nearly eighty additional communities who have identified their need for assistance in addressing local quality issues."[13]

- It is no surprise that a survey of rural communities in New Mexico shows water availability a major problem. That state has officially started a group called the New Mexico Water Dialogue to sensitize citizens to the problems and to promote wise stewardship of this resource.

- On the coast of North Carolina, Dare County (9,100 households), Pamlico County (1,500 households), and Pender County (3,000 households) all have poor quality water.

- Of the fifty neediest communities in Alaska, forty-four have no system of running water.

- A report on Iowa's rural communities notes that "the general problem in about one-half of [these communities] is inadequate quantity and over the entire state quality can be a problem more times than not. . . . Contamination of wells from nitrates and coliform bacteria [is common]."[14]

- In the relatively wealthy state of New York, the "rural water infrastructure is either nonexistent, or dates back to the mid to late 1800s. Many of the systems have not been updated in the last 70 to 100 years. The majority of the existing systems . . . are surface sources without adequate filtration, are contaminated with nitrates, petro chemicals or other sources of pollutants, and are significantly undersized (2 and 4 inch mains)."[15]

- Puerto Rico's 3.5 million people are American citizens, but their status is a residue from the colonial era. They have no U.S. Senators, and one nonvoting member of the national House of Representatives. As a result of their lack of political strength in Congress and in presidential elections, the response to most of their needs, including water problems, is starkly inadequate. Listen to this newspaper account written during a drought:

> Carmen Andino, her hair in curlers and her forehead beaded with perspiration, sits under one of the few shady trees at the housing project where she lives and begins the countdown.
>
> Under a government-imposed rationing plan now entering its fourth month, running water at her home was shut off at 10 A.M. and will not come back on until 10 P.M. the following day—a 36-hour shutdown.
>
> "You can't cook, you can't clean, you can't take a bath," said Andino. "And when the water does come back on, you can't use it for cooking it's so dirty, much less drink it. People are getting sick."
>
> "I've never heard of anything like this outside of an earthquake, a hurricane, a tornado or that sort of thing," said Douglas Short, past chairman of the American Water Works Association's water shortage subcommittee.[16]

- Minnesota may be a land of a thousand lakes, as they boast, but Gaylord, Minnesota, has 717 households without a public water system, and Gaylord is not alone in this Minnesota distinction.

- West Virginia has many natural resources, but its state report for 1995 notes: "Very few areas in the state have good quality ground water."[17] Its report lists 378 communities—that is not a typographical error—with water quality problems. Small wonder that highly respected Senator Robert Byrd said on the floor of the Senate: "The need for eight million Americans to confidently use water for drinking, cooking, and recreation ought to be a birthright. There ought never to be any question about government's doing all that it can in the first place, before there is a crisis, to insure that all Americans have safe drinking water."[18] Who can disagree with that?

- Massachusetts appears to be one of the states least likely to have any type of water difficulty, but Yale University's Paul Kennedy writes: "Coastal shoreline retreat, which . . . is already taking place, will be accelerated by rising sea levels. According to one local study, Massachusetts may lose between three thousand and ten thousand acres of coastal upland by 2025. . . . As coastal bluffs are eroded by higher waves and storm surges, saltwater will move farther upstream and into coastal aquifers, contaminating water supplies at the same time that higher average temperatures create greater demand. Some environmentalists suggest that it is a waste of time and resources to seek to check coastal erosion (by building seawalls, reinforcing the foundations of coastal properties, etc.), but local communities and property owners will obviously press for costly protection and restoration measures."[19]

- Nebraska is the largest user of water from the Ogallala aquifer, a body of water roughly equivalent to Lake Huron, which helps supply water to seven states. Like most underground water sources, the Ogallala is being depleted. More water is pumped from the aquifer each year than is replenished. Perhaps helping to salvage its future is the reality that the remaining water is so deep that pumping it out is becoming more and more expensive.

Concerned citizens have formed the Nebraska Groundwater Foundation. A *National Geographic* study of the area concludes accurately: "However you look at it, the future of the region will be determined, down to its tiniest detail, by the water."[20]

- In 1996 the Texas Water Development Board and the Texas Natural Resource Conservation Commission reported: "The era of plentiful water when an area's needs could be readily met with new water supply development is mostly past."[21] They note that while the demand for water for irrigation will diminish, as development takes more and more land, the demand for water for manufacturing and municipalities will increase, and the water used for irrigation is generally not in the same location as the developing water needs. They add this somber note: "It [is] difficult to marshal the public support needed to bring major new water projects to fruition." A key water researcher in Texas observes: "Given the challenges of continued population growth and increasing competition for water, it's apparent that we have a long way to go."[22]

  Part of the problem in Texas, as in many other places, is the huge disparity in rainfall statewide. El Paso gets about eight inches of rain a year, while the portion of Texas that is along the Louisiana border receives fifty-six inches. Presidio, in the western part of the state, received only 1.6 inches of rain one year while Clarksville, in the northeastern portion of Texas, received 109 inches in twelve months.

  Texas has a greater likelihood of suffering severe drought than most other states. During the Dust Bowl period of the

1930s, Hall County, Texas, went from a population of 40,000 to 1,000. In the 1950s, ninety Texas counties suffered from severe drought conditions—but unlike in the 1930s, the federal government provided emergency help and no similar population shift occurred. Texas is one of only three western states that still does not have a drought plan.

Aquifers in Texas, as in other areas, are being gradually depleted, and those underground resources provide more than half the water used in Texas. It is one of the worst states in the draining of its aquifers. A major source of its water, the Ogallala aquifer, has "two distinctions: one of being the largest discrete [isolated] aquifer in the world, the other of being the fastest-disappearing aquifer in the world."[23] From 1930 to 1980, water use in Texas increased almost six times, while the state population only tripled.

· · ·

Is the future hopeless in Florida, Texas, and other states? Not if we start addressing the problems with long-range answers now.

5

THE MIDDLE EAST

The Koran has words that no Christian or Jewish leader of the Middle East would dispute: "We made from water everything."[1] The words sound ominous when combined with a World Bank report on that region: "Within one lifetime (1960 to 2025), per capita renewable [water] supplies will have fallen [annually] from 3,430 cubic meters to 667 cubic meters."[2]

I have traveled many times by air and by car through the Middle East, and the overall impression is that of dryness and the dominance of desert brown.

Shortly after the late Yitzhak Rabin became Prime Minister of Israel, he visited the United States and met with several of us from the Senate Foreign Relations Committee. My colleagues asked him about relations with Syria and other international tensions, and I asked him about water and the needs of his nation and the region. Prime Minister Rabin, an unusually low-key speaker and conversationalist for a public official, suddenly displayed more passion than on any other subject.

"You probably did not know," he said, "that before I entered the military, I was a water engineer. If we solve every other problem in the Middle East but do not satisfactorily resolve the water problem, our region will explode. Peace will not be possible." He spoke of the need for desalination and later asked me to join the regional water talks taking place, one of five separate areas being addressed then by Middle East leaders, this one presided over by the United States. Because of the Senate schedule, I could not accept his invitation. The group has had six meetings since its initial encounter in 1992, with Israel, Jordan, and the Palestinians among the active participants; and Syria and Lebanon (under Syria's thumb) are nonparticipants. The fact that forty-four other countries attended as observers illustrates the importance that other nations see in these water talks. All of these nations are there because they understand that agreement on water is essential for a stable Middle East.

Almost every leader in that region has said: Solving the water problem is essential to the future of the area.

In 1985 Boutros Boutros-Ghali, later secretary-general of the United Nations but then foreign minister of Egypt, prophesied: "The next war in the Middle East will be fought over water, not politics."[3] He added: "Washington doesn't take this seriously, because everything for the United States relates to oil."[4] Days before President Anwar Sadat signed the peace treaty with Israel, he said, "The only matter that could take Egypt to war again is water."[5] King Hussein of Jordan observed that water is the one issue that "could drive nations of the region to war."[6] A feature story in *National Geographic* on the Middle East speaks of a region "where growing nations compete for a shrinking water supply."[7] It talks about "a crisis in the making." Former U.S. Secretary of State Warren Christopher writes: "In the parched valleys of the Middle East . . . the struggle for water has a direct impact on security and stability."[8] A few weeks after he took office as prime minister, Benjamin Netanyahu told me: "Israel is headed toward a mess in water."[9] What has been a serious problem for several decades will become much more critical. One study concludes simply: "The region is running out of water."[10]

In 1993 Shimon Peres, then the Israeli foreign minister, wrote a book, *The New Middle East.* Much of it is devoted to the volatile subject of water. He begins one chapter: "A Jewish saying goes as follows: All the miracles that God granted the people of Israel were involved with water. Water is scarce in our torrid region of the world. . . . The region's water shortage had a strong impact on Islamic architecture, and contributed to the Muslim practice of placing many large-roomed cool buildings around a large central courtyard that held the wells. Water is an essential part of Jewish, Christian, and Moslem rituals, such as washing of the hands (Jews), baptism (Christians), and washing of the feet (Muslims). . . . Water continues to be a key consideration in modern political policy. Relationships among the countries of the region . . . continue to be dictated largely by water policy. . . . A serious violation of water rights is sometimes recognized as justification for war."[11]

Every leader of a Middle East nation can talk knowledgeably about water. Almost no leaders in the United States can talk knowledgeably about water, yet for solutions to be achieved in this vital field, the United States must lead.

What most Americans do not know, or fail to remember, is that many of the skirmishes between Israel and her Arab neighbors

. . . .

either have been fights over water or battles that began initially over water. After Israel's independence in 1948, the Arab states and Israel signed an uneasy armistice that did not deal with water issues. But two years later, when Israel started to drain the Hialeah swamps, Syria claimed this violated the demilitarized zone between Israel and Syria, and several military incidents occurred. Many more followed over the Sea of Galilee (also called Lake Tiberias or Lake Kinneret) and other water resources.

President Dwight Eisenhower's special envoy, Eric Johnston, appointed in 1953, developed a regional water plan to which the nations of the area did not agree but which they generally followed. President Eisenhower launched the study because of the series of border clashes between Israel and Syria over water in 1951. Israel developed a National Water Carrier plan in 1953 (completed in 1964), which stayed within the limitations of the Johnston proposal, moving water from the northern part of Israel to the water-deficient south. Neighboring Arab nations, accurately seeing this as one step toward the healthy development of Israel, agreed on a plan to divert some of the headwaters of the Upper Jordan, depriving Israel of about 35 percent of its anticipated withdrawal from that source, and almost half of the water to be transported by Israel's National Water Carrier. Because the Arab nations did not sign the Johnston plan, they believed that they were within their international rights to divert the water. Israel saw this as a threat to its survival and, in April 1967, launched a series of air strikes, climaxed by an attack well into the interior of Syria.

Two months later, the Arab nations responded by launching the Six-Day War, initiated by passion and centuries of enmity, but fueled by problems over water. The war left Egypt, Jordan, and Syria with less territory and Israel with a greater sense of security, but with basic, long-term difficulties still festering, water being a prime example. Israel's hawkish political leader, Ariel Sharon, a former general, told a reporter: "People generally regard June 5, 1967, as the day the Six-Day War began. That is the official date, but in reality it started two-and-one-half years earlier on the day Israel decided to act against the diversion of the Jordan."[12]

Writing about the Middle East, environmental journalist Jessica Matthews observes: "No resource, including oil, is a sharper spur to conflict than water."[13] A Canadian specialist on the region writes: "Contrary to a widely held view in the West, the most highly prized resource in the Middle East is not oil but water."[14] Of 286 international water agreements, only one is in the Middle East, an agreement between Sudan and Egypt on the Nile—two of nine nations on that river. The World Bank calls the water problems of the Middle East "among the most urgent, complex, and intractable of any region in the world."[15] In 1975 Syria and Iraq almost went to war over water. In the 1992 Persian Gulf War, water supply facilities in both Iraq and Kuwait were targets because both sides knew that without water the opposition would crumble. Water played a role in the steps that led to that conflict. Iraq wanted Kuwait's northern islands, Bubiyan and Warbah, because of Iraq's desire for deep seaports. Iraq pledged to supply Kuwait with freshwater if the islands would be ceded to Iraq, but the al-Sabah family, which rules Kuwait, turned back Iraq's frequent entreaties.

In 1995 syndicated columnist Jay Bushinsky wrote from Jerusalem: "Years ago, Senator Paul Simon called the attention of the U.S. Congress to a problem that could be mankind's undoing: the uneven and sometimes wasteful distribution of water for agriculture, industry and direct human consumption." Bushinsky said more and more leaders are now agreeing with "Simon's dire forecast," particularly in the Middle East.[16] It took—and takes—

no great skill or foresight to know that nation after nation and region after region are headed for great trouble, and the situation the Middle East faces is the most serious. An extreme example is tiny Djibouti, the world's most water-scarce nation, with about 4,800 gallons of water available per capita for a year, compared to 35,000 times that amount available in water-rich Iceland.

But a look at the larger Middle East nations, and the growing dependence they have on one another, illustrates the need for great concern.

Turkey is developing the Anatolia Project, which includes twenty-two dams and nineteen power plants that take advantage of the Tigris and Euphrates Rivers, as well as a huge dam 340 miles southeast of Ankara named for the Turkish revolutionary leader Attaturk. That project has the potential to reduce the flow of the Euphrates into Syria and Iraq by as much as 60 percent. Turkey is the water giant and the military giant of the three nations. Syria, once a food-exporting country but now a food importer, and Iraq, already short of water, would suffer dramatic reductions in agricultural production if Turkey should fully exercise that option. Turkey is planning more irrigation, and that probably will mean less water for Syria and Iraq and almost certainly water that is higher in saline content as well. The three nations are trying to work out an agreement, but few are optimistic that will happen, though there is a general expectation that Turkey will act responsibly. But the potential for an explosion is always on the minds of area leaders. Turkey has barren areas, but compared to other nations in the region has relatively small problems and much slower population growth projected than for other countries. Turkey' population is expected to increase from its current 63 million to 77 million by the year 2010.

Adding to the severity of the situation is the fact that Syria, which is 70 percent desert, will increase its population by 50 percent by the end of the next decade, going from 15 million to 23 million. Syria has an astounding growth rate of 3.8 percent a year. It is dependent on water for electricity, and the reduced flow of water from the Euphrates into Syria means that Damascus and other cities frequently are without electricity. "Only two of the [Euphrates] dam's eight turbines are working," observes a Syrian Immigration Ministry official. "There has never been enough water for them all."[17] Amazingly, until 1996, Damascus had no water purification system. This city had 300,000 people in 1960 and now has 3 million. Its city engineer notes: "We have to find new sources of water, and we have to clean whatever water passes through the city so it can be reused in the gardens and orchards."[18]

Downstream from Turkey and Syria is Iraq, concerned about a dwindling water supply as the population rises. Iraq is 75 percent desert and will go from 20 million to 31 million by the end of the next decade. Twenty percent of Iraq is farmland, half of which has enough rain to grow crops. The other half is almost totally dependent on the flow from rivers for irrigation. To Iraqi complaints about Syrian use of Euphrates water, Syrian officials point to their own population growth and ask, "What can we do? We have to take care of our people." Complicating Syria's—and indirectly Iraq's—problems further, the Quwayq River, which once helped provide Syria with drinking water, has dried up, as farmers now use its headwaters for irrigation.

Egypt's serious problems will worsen considerably because this nation, with almost 100 percent of its land covered by desert, is expected to grow from 62 million people to 81 million by 2010 and is almost totally dependent on the Nile, whose headwaters it does not control. Eighty-five percent of the flow of the Nile originates in Ethiopia, which is now recovering from decades of bad government. Unfortunately, the gradual improvement in the quality of life of the Ethiopians and a burgeoning population mean an increase in its use of water. Ethiopia is considering construction of a hydroelectric dam on the river, causing at least temporary problems for the rest of the river nations, particularly Egypt. "The national security of Egypt is in the hands of eight other African countries in the Nile basin," Boutros-Ghali, then an Egyptian cabinet member, said in 1989.[19] The Nile, the world's longest river, wanders through eight nations before it reaches Egypt. Any additional consumption of water along the route threatens the life of Egypt—more than 95 percent of the Nile's water flows into it from other nations. Ninety-nine percent of Egypt's food production comes from irrigated land. "Beyond 2000 our water [situation] is very dark and very serious," an Egyptian official notes.[20] Over the centuries Egypt has been enriched by the deposits from the Nile, which have made its soil fertile. The English word *chemistry* comes from these deposits, considered once to have all essential substances. But the Aswan Dam, which is of great help in controlling floods in Egypt and assuring a more regular water supply, diminishes those rich deposits and increases the salinity of the deposits it leaves. The Nile no longer washes out the salt residue through floods along the banks of the river. In 1997 President Hosni Mubarak dedicated a canal in the Sahara in western Egypt near Lake Nasser, which was created by the Aswan Dam, called the Toshka Project. Its purpose is to create a new Upper Egypt Valley. The project, costing well over $2 billion, could help agriculture and make part of a desert area green. It may turn out to be a great asset to Egypt, carrying water to parched land—or this diversion could complicate all of Egypt's water problems, making less water available in other areas, depending on whose forecast is accepted. Egypt is potentially a food exporter, if its water shortage can be solved, but now it must import almost half of its food.

Jordan is 70 percent desert, and its population of 4.1 million will reach 7.9 million by 2010. It shares the Jordan River with Israel, and many Jordanian citizens complain that Israel takes too much water. But if Israel took no water, Jordan would still face a crisis in a few years. The Yarmuk, a tributary of the Jordan, is shared with Syria and Israel. The only river Jordan can call its own that flows entirely within the country is the tiny Zarqa. Jordan's mushrooming capital city, Amman, rations water. The metal tanks atop homes for salvaging water, which visitors see occasionally in other countries, are everywhere in Amman. Jordan is adopting many of Israel's water-saving technologies, but the prospects for Jordan are grim. A growing population is consuming more water and eating more food, putting greater demand on already water-starved agriculture. Add the factor of a higher standard of living, which ordinarily means consuming even more water, and a poor sewage system, and you understand the deep concern of Jordanian leaders. In 1991 effluent from industry and a bad sewer system combined to severely damage 15,000 acres of irrigated vegetable crops.

I first visited Israel and Jordan in 1957 as a young journalist. The huge changes since that time, including an improved quality of life, are evident in both nations. But the difference in appearance of the landscape is particularly dramatic in Israel. Israel literally has made the desert bloom, including many areas like the Rift Valley south of the Dead Sea, which experts "previously considered too arid for cultivation."[21] The Israelis have applied their considerable scientific skills to reduce per capita water consumption, but they know there is a crisis ahead. Of one of its major sources of water, the Jordan River, Shimon Peres once commented that it "has more history in it than water."[22] One American writer describes the famed Jordan River this way: "It runs a total of barely 200 miles. It is smaller than the Platte, the Connecticut, and the Delaware. More water flows down the Nile in a week than comes down the Jordan in a year."[23] Yet in terms of this parched, overpopulated region, its waters are desperately needed and frequently disputed. California has a water problem, yet that state has eight times more water per capita than Israel.

Israel's principal sources of water, other than the Jordan River, are the Yarmuk River and overused underground aquifers, from which Israel gets about 40 percent of its water. Equally as famous as the Jordan is the Sea of Galilee. Although it is healthy, its salinity is too high to use on citrus crops or for many other agricultural needs. Approximately 70 percent of Israel's water is used for agricultural production, which accounts for less than 5 percent of its national income. But understandably, Israel does not want to become dependent on others for food. If a significant breakthrough in the cost of desalination occurs, Israel views the agricultural sector as rapidly growing in economic importance because of the increasing population of Israel and her neighbors.

In 1995 Israel's National Water Authority issued a statement: "Water resources are being depleted and storage facilities are insufficient to meet future demand. . . . The mass influx of new immigrants from the former Soviet Union and the overall population increase have increased water consumption to the point that all resources are being utilized to the maximum. . . . Even in the event of plentiful rainfall, which fully replenishes the aquifers, the overall storage capacity is still less than current demand. . . . In Jerusalem, demand jumped by nearly 21 percent and in Beersheba by 24 percent since 1992. . . . Demand for freshwater in small and medium-sized towns has rocketed by an average of over 32 percent in the past four years."[24]

Israel is 35 percent desert, and its population of 5.1 million will go to 6.8 million by 2010. Issues of quality and quantity cannot be totally separated in Israel or anywhere else. Israel has the highest quality standards in the Middle East, yet drinking water is tolerated with seventy milligrams of nitrates per liter, compared to forty-five milligrams per liter permitted in the United States and Western Europe. Israel's lower standards are necessitated in part by declining aquifers. Complicating Israel's situation is that only half of its sewage is treated. In 1985 people in the suburbs of Haifa experienced serious digestive diseases, causing more than 10,000 to become ill and two to die, the most serious event of its type in Israeli history. The mass illnesses that lasted only two weeks were caused by sewage water entering the Ofek II well, which supplies water to the area.[25] Because of quantity and quality problems, Israelis drink less water than their American friends and, as a result, are nine times more likely to have kidney stone problems than citizens of the United States.[26]

Israel's problems generally are much fewer than in the rest of the Middle East. Children are particularly susceptible to water-borne diseases, and the Middle East has the highest percentage of children under the age of fourteen—43 percent of the population—of any region outside of sub-Saharan Africa.

Political agreements with neighboring Arab countries are essential to Israel for the assurance of water, but complicate Israel's future because some of the water resources temporarily under Israeli control have shifted back to Palestinian hands. Roughly one-third of Israel's water supply is tied to territory it occupied after the 1967 War. That complicates every problem.

An American journalist reported from Jerusalem: "The attitudes of Israelis (fear) and Palestinians (anger and resentment) on the issue of water are a stark illustration of why peace talks on extending Palestinian autonomy to the West Bank have proceeded at a snail's pace. . . . The anxiety is worsened by the knowledge that water is scarce all over the region, with poor quality adding to the problem of insufficient quantity."[27] She writes about a Palestinian truck driver who "delivers his goods to nearby homes and businesses. His cargo is water, and his price is $6 a cubic meter (264 gallons), more than four times what the municipality charges. But his clients are glad to have it at any price because the water taps in Bethlehem, as in many other West Bank towns, frequently contain nothing but hot air." Jericho sometimes has drinking water available only one day a week. Even with cooperation from Arab neighbors, Israel's water future is grim; without cooperation, it could be catastrophic. Israel's water needs are expected to be 30 percent greater than supply within a few years.

The Gaza Strip is only 140 square miles and has 900,000 people, a population density of 6,500 people per square mile. It has probably the highest birth rate in the world and its population grows 5.1 percent a year. By 2010 its population will double. It has severe water problems—and severe problems of almost every variety—but it also has a population with a higher average educational attainment than most areas of the world and the potential to develop a port in a key part of that region.

The only nation in the Middle East that does not face serious water problems is Lebanon, and ironically, Lebanon is the only nation in the area that is not expected to experience population growth in the near future. Lebanon's population of 3.7 million is expected to be about the same at the end of the next decade.

It has virtually no desert. Lebanon does have water and sewage systems badly damaged by the conflicts that paralyzed the nation for a period, plus those that deteriorated because of age. The south of Lebanon is occupied by Shiites, who are poorer than the Christians, Sunnis, and Druze. The Shiites receive less water for irrigation and other purposes and less attention. They claim to be treated unfairly, a claim that may be accurate. However, Lebanon's water difficulties are much more easily solved than those of the rest of the region. Lebanon's cooperation in resolving problems can be critical to other nations, but without Syria's nonpublic nod of approval that is not probable.

A quick look at Saudi Arabia reveals overwhelming problems: 18 million people today, and a projected 28 million by 2010; the largest sand desert in the world within a nation that is 92 percent desert; no rivers that flow year-round; deep underground aquifers that are being depleted; an average of only four inches of rain a year; and less than 2 percent of its total land under cultivation. The long-run water picture is not bright, but that is only part of the story. No nation in the region has turned things around as much as Saudi Arabia, with the exception of Israel. Two decades ago, the Saudis were net food importers; today they are exporters. Orchards and vegetable farms, dairies and chicken farms are now part of the landscape. The Saudis quadrupled food production in twenty years. Land under cultivation mushroomed in thirteen years from less than 400,000 acres to more than 8 million acres. Reserves of wheat are being stockpiled for a nonrainy day. Most important, the nutritional intake of the Saudi people has improved. The key to all of this is water from aquifers and water that is desalinated, reused, and conserved. The Saudis started desalination in 1938 and shortly will produce 800 million gallons of it a day. Two-thirds of the water consumed in

Riyadh, their largest city, is desalinated seawater, and nationally, the desalinated water is approximately 20 percent of total consumption. Most of the groundwater that is used must be treated to remove salt. (It is also worth noting that no nation is helping other countries with foreign economic assistance as much as Saudi Arabia. The United States contributes about .13 percent of our national income to international development aid, and the western European nation giving the most is Norway at 1.16 percent, while the Saudis contribute 3.9 percent. Much of that advances their political agenda, but that is true of efforts by many nations, including the United States.)

While the Middle East offers striking examples of problems the world will soon face, it also offers lessons to be learned. These lessons are not strikingly different from those to be learned in other regions. Shimon Peres concludes one chapter in a book: "If roads lead to civilization, then water leads to peace."[28]

Or to war.

6

OTHER NATIONS

While the Middle East is the most immediately volatile of the places where water shortages could provoke misery and war, the litany of nations that will soon face critical situations is unfortunately lengthy. Their future is tied to ours, as humanity is inextricably intertwined.

The World Bank lists twenty-two nations as having *severe* water problems. Eighty nations have *serious* water problems. As the world's population grows, the picture will become more and more grim. And it is not only the sweeping world picture, it is also the disparity between nations and within nations that adds agony.

In developing nations, the shortage of water and bad distribution systems are particularly hard on women and children. They tend to be "the beasts of burden" who carry water from the supply point to where a family lives. Children often do not attend school because they must carry water. Women who are pregnant or sick find little sympathy or relief from their water duty in the traditions of many nations. Walking miles for water each day is common. Visitors to developing nations may find scenes of women hauling large containers filled with water on their heads picturesque, but those who carry the water have a far different perspective.

The Tonfiou (phonetic spelling) family in Senegal lives in a small cluster of houses, probably too small to be called a village. They do have a village elder but apparently no formal structure. The Tonfious, like other people there, carry water about four miles, a long walk in the hot sun with a heavy burden of water. There are four children in the family, and the two oldest, a daughter and a son, have left to try for a better life in Dakar, the capital city. "My daughter got tired of carrying water," the father explains simply about her leaving home. The two have added to the growing urban population and problems of Dakar, and have visited home once since leaving more than eight months earlier, dressed in clothes their younger sisters admired. The father, apparently speaking for his wife also, has serious misgivings about their going to the big city. "If we only had water here they would have stayed," he said. That's only one family in a world of almost 6 billion people, but it is a story repeated over and over and over again.

Specialists talk about "a basic water requirement" for humanity to survive. Estimates are from twenty to forty liters (a liter is slightly more than a quart) per day for drinking, sanitation, and hygiene, the figure varying according to the expert and the climate in which people live. Water specialist Peter Gleick believes—correctly—that food preparation and bathing should be included, and his recommendation is a basic fifty liters per day, for national and international planning purposes. Twenty-six nations already fall beneath the low twenty-liter standard and an additional twenty-nine nations fall below the Gleick standard. Examples of the need for more water are everywhere.

Mexico's population is 90 million and is expected to reach 154 million in less than thirty years. Population growth will compound all the problems of water-hungry Mexico, and what they confront is already serious. Mexico City, one of the world's largest urban concentrations, is depleting its main aquifer by more than ten feet a year. It now pumps water from as far as 120 miles away, which escalates costs about 55 percent, and that is only a small hint at what awaits Mexico City in the decades ahead.

Everyone who follows the international scene knows about Mexico's peso crisis of 1994, and its loan from the United States to ease an economic crisis. Our leaders responded properly, recognizing that deterioration of the situation in Mexico could do great harm to our country.

Much less well known is that a few months afterward, Mexico made another loan request—for 2.8 million cubic meters of water from the Rio Grande River. Sandra Postel, director of the Global Water Policy Project in Amherst, Massachusetts, and a leading U.S. water generalist, describes the cause of this request and what happened:

Much of northern Mexico was in the third year of a drought that had already killed crops and cattle. Rising salt levels in the river were killing fish and other aquatic life. . . . Mexico had used all but about 5 percent of its share of reservoir water set by a 1944 treaty with the United States, so the nation was facing even greater losses if it did not get additional supplies. Although the U.S. government had just a few months earlier promised Mexico $20 billion to shore up its economy, it decided against the water loan. It deferred to the concerns of Texas that a loan to Mexico might leave Texan farmers without enough water for themselves.[1]

Nothing calamitous happened as a result of the U.S. cold shoulder to the Mexican request. But double Mexico's population and add that to soil that is much, much "thirstier," and you will either have a government there that may threaten military action, or you will have massive movement of a desperate population to its relatively water-rich northern neighbor. You can have border patrols, thirty-foot-high fences, and other barriers, but people who see their families threatened by extinction will go under, through, and around the fences or go by boat to survive. The illegal immigration tides that the United States experiences from Mexico today are tiny compared to the influx a parched Mexico will bring us.

The demand for water—and clean water—in Mexico is so clear and huge and growing that Coca-Cola and Pepsi Cola are investing millions to install bottled water machines all over the nation.

Under terms of a 1944 treaty, the United States currently guarantees Mexico 1.5 million acre-feet of water a year from the Colorado River, and to assure its quality, the U.S. built a desalination plant in Yuma, Arizona, which operates when needed. The Mexicali Valley of thirsty Mexico is heavily dependent on the Colorado River water. The rising demand in both the southwestern United States and Mexico spells trouble for the future, even without considering the problem of groundwater depletion. Few agreements exist between nations on aquifer use, and how to monitor and apportion it. Depleting of aquifers is almost certain to add increased tension to water disagreements. Thirty miles south of Mexico City developers planned to spend $300 million in 1996 on a golf course in the picturesque town of Tepoztian. Local citizens complained vigorously it would take their water. The protests grew violent. Twenty people suffered injuries and police killed one man. A small incident, but an incident that could portend what will happen in much of the world.

Most water disputes between nations will not result in military action, but some will. Where there are already tensions between nations, water difficulties will accentuate and heighten the tensions. Contrary to the public perception, few wars start over one incident, but one incident can trigger an explosion between two nations with tense relations. I visited Honduras and El Salvador shortly after their "Soccer War" of 1969. Media coverage suggested that the teams of the two nations played, and then the melee afterward escalated into a shooting war. It is true that the soccer game triggered the war, but relations between the two nations had deteriorated badly long before the athletic contest. Most conflicts over water will be settled peacefully, despite the difficult situation severe water shortages will create. But where two nations maintain a civil but sour relationship, water could easily cause an eruption of bloodshed. The stakes are high when something essential to survival is threatened, and in many instances, countries neighboring the two contestants will be sucked into military involvement.

The World Bank, the United Nations, and various research groups project that as many as eighty nations will face *severe* water shortages by the end of the next two decades. But even that does not tell the full story.

China, for example, is not among the nations ordinarily listed, because if you take the total water supply of China and divide it by the population projections, China escapes the severe forecasts.

However, China is not awash in water. With 21 percent of the world's population, it has only 8 percent of our earth's renewable freshwater. The difficulty in China, as in the United States and many countries, is that water is not spread out evenly. In our country we have areas of difficulty, described in earlier chapters, even though we have almost five times as much water available per capita as China. But just as getting water from Michigan to Nevada is not easy, getting that vital liquid from one remote area of China to an area of great shortage is also not easy. Further complicating the problem, China does not have our financial resources for solving its problems, even though its per capita water consumption is lower than that of most nations.

Where China's leadership is going remains unclear. A widely read recent book, *The Coming Conflict with China*, by Richard Bernstein and Ross Munro, suggests its leadership may emerge fairly militant. Even if that is not their *intent*, historically, one of the ways political leaders—particularly dictators—solve problems of domestic unrest is to create outside enemies. The last thing the world needs is an unstable China. But growing water problems will not help. I have met with intellectual leaders in China who are extremely concerned about China's water future and what will happen to the course of that nation if increasing problems are not satisfactorily resolved. Not as well known as the Bernstein-Munro book, cited above, is an equally important book by Lester Brown, *Who Will Feed China?* In it he points to the population and water crunch that China will soon face, a nation with a growing population, growing influence, and growing problems.

The Yellow River (Huang He), which used to run into the Yellow Sea, is often dry now before it reaches the sea. In 1995 it became dry more than 400 miles from the Yellow Sea. China already has more than 300 cities that are short of water, and one-third of them face severe problems. Additionally, cropland that is vital to China's people is gradually losing some of its water support. The following 1996 *New York Times* story is the type of article that will appear with increasing frequency:

LITINGZHUANG, China—The one time this spring that there was actually enough water in the Yellow River to flow all the way to its mouth on the Bohai Sea, the peasants in this village of brick and mud homes were not allowed to use it.

Just a month away from the summer wheat harvest, the farmers here were forced to stand by as hundreds of millions of gallons of water flowed past their thirsty crops to a state-run oil field downstream at Dongying. The oil company's directors had pleaded to Communist Party officials in Beijing that without the water they would be forced to shut down crucial pumping operations.

Tempers flared and earthy epithets flew when the peasants discovered that guards had been stationed at the valves to their fields. . . .

What happened along the lower reaches of the Yellow River this spring was another portent of China's developing water crisis.[2]

In northern China, the water levels of the aquifers are dropping steadily. In the Beijing area, depleted underground water supplies have caused some ground subsidence. More of the same is expected.

Crisis will build upon crisis in China with considerable unrest if the world's policymakers do not move toward sensible, long-range answers. When a nation with more than one-fifth of the world's population experiences instability, strong shock waves are likely to be felt everywhere.

The disparity of water supply within nations and between

nations makes many of the statistical studies meaningless. On paper many nations have enough water. Australia—the driest continent— has water in abundance in some areas and desperate shortages in others. Despite addressing its needs in a comprehensive fashion since 1914, Australia's leaders understand they are heading for difficulties. The Murray-Darling river system is Australia's most important, but salinization of the soil is increasing due to higher levels of salinity in the rivers. At some places in its valley large clumps of salt are visible on the land. One report notes: "Not only soils are salt-affected; the water in virtually all of the wheat-belt streams has become too salty for human consumption."[3] Despite Australia's water-related problems due to shortfalls, it has water-related potential that could be important to that nation and to the growing world population. It has at least 20 million acres available, which could be producing food, if they had a water supply.

Bangladesh has more than enough water to last a year—in theory—but unfortunately most of it comes at one time, with huge flooding; then much of the rest of the year that impoverished nation experiences a drought. Significant population growth will make Bangladesh's difficulties much worse. The nation's 110 million people will grow to approximately 200 million in less than three decades.

I am old enough to remember that when we talked about food needs and starving people, India served as the prime example. Today India is not only self-sufficient, but a food exporter. The difficult, long-range question is whether India has achieved that status in part as a result of over-exploitation of water.

India theoretically has an adequate per capita water supply nationally, but the state of Rajasthan receives only 20 percent as much rainfall as the rest of the nation and has very limited water availability from other sources. In 1974, in another case, India and

Bangladesh agreed on the allocation of the waters of the Ganges, but in 1988 the agreement ended and serious water disputes resulted. The river is 1,300 miles long and affects the lives of 500 million people. After the agreement fell apart, Bangladesh found itself with one-fifth as much water in some areas, dramatically reducing food production, and the reduced flows of the Ganges caused seawater and its salt to penetrate as much as fifty miles inland, damaging the soil further. The issue was nearing the explosion point when a new Indian prime minister, I. K. Gujral, came to office who resolved to improve that nation's relations with Pakistan and Bangladesh. In December 1996, India and Bangladesh reached an agreement. In the future those agreements will be much more difficult to achieve, as population rises and per capita water availability diminishes.

Another snapshot from India will unfortunately be duplicated in other nations: "In the summer of 1988, millions in Delhi went without water during the drought; when the rains finally arrived, wells were polluted by human feces that are everywhere (because of the inadequate sewage system), and a cholera epidemic broke out among the poor."[4]

More than 10 million food-producing acres in India have been lost to salinization because of improper irrigation. And India gets most of its food production from irrigated land.

A study of the sustainability of groundwater in the state of Gujarat in India found it "declining alarmingly." Groundwater is the source of 77 percent of the irrigation for that state.[5] Of ninety-six wells monitored over a ten-year period, eighty-seven showed drops in the water level of twenty-two to thirty feet. Gujarat had less than 4 percent of its households served with electricity at the time of Indian independence in 1947. Today 97 percent have electricity, but that good news also means that farmers can use electric pumps to extract water for irrigation much more easily. Equally bad news: Farmers in Gujarat are charged a flat fee, no matter how much electricity they use. There is no reason for them not to keep the electric pumps running far beyond need.

More than 8,000 villages in India have no local water supply. In the state of Tamil Nadu, diverting water from the Bhavani River for industrial expansion is understandable, but that means that many rural areas cannot be served. In the breadbasket states of Punjab and Haryana water tables are falling. In India, China, Senegal, and many other nations, growing demands for water for the cities require reaching out farther and farther for water, often depriving rural areas of their sources.

In Pakistan, the coordinator of the National Conservation Strategy is concerned about the survival of the land and the people because of the country's water deficiencies. He adds: "I know of nine-year-old farm lads in jail for murder over water disputes." Those nine-year-olds may be symbols of the future, not just in Pakistan, but in much of the world.

In Thailand the important Chao Phraya basin faces frequent water shortages, and the aquifer below the capital city of Bangkok is dropping rapidly.

Visitors to Manila may have difficulty believing that the Philippines can have water shortages despite the frequent rains there. However, in December 1997, the government cut Manila's water use to less than twelve hours a day, and the General Hospital had to postpone surgical operations because of the lack of water.

As the water-poor nations use more and more of their underground water resources, disparities grow, and as salinity creeps in, the trouble with water quantity is worsened by deteriorating quality. Water-borne diseases hobble a nation or a region, and children are particularly susceptible to those attacks. Malaria, once a declining threat to the world, now is making a dramatic resurgence.

While the isolated stories of individual nations related in this chapter may seem unconnected, the individual pieces of this mosaic form a picture that is devastating. A small-circulation periodical that is devoted to defense questions, *International Security*, has two major articles on water under the general heading, "Will Blood Flow for H_2O?"[6] Their conclusions are not comforting. But even in the unlikely event that water shortages do not lead to wars, they will lead to massive misery.

"Forget about the Turks. Water is our biggest problem!" says a Cyprus official of the Ministry of Agriculture.[7] While Cyprus has a relatively efficient irrigation system, in January 1997 the seventeen largest reservoirs in the nation were only 20 percent full and the saltwater seepage increasingly threatened the gradually depleted groundwater resources. The good news is that although totally dependent until recently on rainfall, more than nine-tenths of the residents of the island now have piped water for drinking. But the population is growing. Cyprus's hopes rest on four desalination plants under construction, one of which went into partial operation in May 1997. The expectation is that that plant will meet the water demands of the southeast portion of the island, including most of the 2 million tourists who visit Cyprus each year. Only 734,000 people live on the island year-round, which is divided by a "green line" maintained by the United Nations between the Greek and Turkish sides. There is virtually no traffic and communication between the two sides. When Israel and Jordan were theoretically in a declared state of war with each other, more traffic crossed that border in a day than crosses the Cyprus green line in a year. But it is not an isolated island. Citizens of Greece and Turkey have deep emotional commitments to the two sides. If water troubles develop into armed confrontation in Cyprus, Greece and Turkey are not likely to remain aloof. Politically, no government of either Greece or Turkey could survive if it failed to defend the security and interests of "their" people in Cyprus.

Greece has a slowly growing population, a rapidly growing tourist trade, and environmental problems that include water shortages and a declining quality of water. Excessive use of groundwater to meet deficiencies is causing saltwater invasion of aquifers. Athens relies heavily on underground water, which is being depleted and becoming more and more salty. More than 80 percent of Greece's water supply is used for irrigation. One-third of Greece's irrigated farmland is now crippled by saline deposits. Adding to that nation's difficulties, only 10 percent of sewage is treated, with most of the runoff going directly into the sea. That, plus agricultural chemical fertilizers combined with industrial runoffs, causes Greece—rich in coastline—to produce only one-tenth of one percent of the world's fish catch.[8] As to those small dots on the map near Greece, one study concludes: "In most of the Greek islands the water situation ranges from bad to truly distressing."[9]

Mauritania, on the western coast of North Africa, has 2.3 million people and 375 miles of coastline. One of the most striking scenes for a visitor is seeing how the desert creeps right up to the city limits of the small capital, Nouakchott. The main highway in the nation can be traversed only by camel or four-wheel-drive vehicles, because frequently the wind blows the sand over the road. (I have traveled that highway only once—and I do not want to do it again.) People desperate for wood for fuel chop down the scrubby trees that border the desert and somehow have survived, but as the trees go, the desert grows. And that brings more problems. During the entire decade of the 1960s, stinging sandstorms lashed Mauritania forty-three times. Now many times that number beat down upon the people and environment there *each year*. Less dramatic than the growth of the desert at the doorstep of the capital city and other cities is the creep of the desert onto agricultural and grazing lands. In a bad year, Mauritania grows only 8 percent of its food. This spread of the desert sent nomadic Arab herders south, causing the Mauritania-Senegal conflict of 1989, when the herders clashed with black, nonnomadic farmers on both sides of the Senegal River, which divides the two countries. While a drought harmed Mauritania in the 1980s, the nation will need 40 percent more water simply for rural drinking purposes in the next few years. What all of these demands on the shriveling supply will mean for growing crops and for grazing—and for security with her neighbors—is only speculation. But all the speculation is negative.

In Kenya, in Ghana, in more than 100 developing nations, part of the reason for the huge growth of urban populations—Nairobi in Kenya grew more than 600 percent in one decade—is that village wells run dry, tillable land turns to desert, and many have no choice but to move to the city if they wish to survive. Others, like the children in the Tonfiou family described at the beginning of the chapter, choose urban life because they do not want to spend a good portion of their lives hauling water.

In 1991 the United Nations Development Program convened an international meeting of poor nations in the Netherlands to talk about Third World water problems. The conclusion of the conference: a new strategy for water is desperately needed for the next century. In addition to critical shortages that nations—and particularly urban areas—will face, the report of the conference stressed that water-related diseases are taking an increasing toll among children, particularly in the poorer nations. In Peru, polluted water brought on a cholera epidemic that cost the nation more than $1 billion in economic losses—not counting its human toll—several times as much as Peru invested in improving its water system in a decade. This is Peter Gleick's testimony about deteriorating water and its health impact: "In 1990, 71,000 cases of cholera were reported to the World Health Organization; none came from Latin America. . . . One year later, in 1991, cholera exploded in the region, with over 390,000 cases reported in fourteen Latin American countries alone, and over 590,000 cases worldwide."[10]

Britain's most widely read magazine in the United States, *The Economist*, asked the basic question that many nations will soon face: "What if there is simply not enough water, however managed, to support population growth in some countries?"[11] Those words appeared in 1992, when too few of the world's leaders had the looming water crisis even remotely on their political agendas. More leaders and scholars now are at least vaguely aware of what lies ahead, but their numbers still are far too few, and urgent short-term problems receive more attention than larger, long-term difficulties. That is one of the weaknesses of politics in almost all nations.

But even short-term water quantity and quality problems must be addressed. For example, in Surabaya, Indonesia's second largest city, large numbers of its citizens must buy water from vendors at prices that are as much as ten times higher than what they would pay for water from a piped system. And vendors supply water of questionable quality. In the capital city of Jakarta, with 8 million people, only 14 percent of the population receives piped water directly. One-third purchase water from street vendors and the remainder have wells—the latter two categories presenting major quality problems in a city with more than 800,000 septic tanks that sometimes work and sometimes don't.

Singapore, one of the "economic miracle" nations of Asia, is totally dependent on Malaysia for water. Any deterioration of the relationship between these two nations could cause huge problems for Singapore.

Far from Singapore is Haiti, where impoverished families spend as much as 20 percent of their meager income on water. Some of the Caribbean islands already have lost industrial development opportunities because of water limitations, and as their populations grow, the development opportunities will decline further.

Droughts exacerbate already difficult situations that nations face from North Korea to Ethiopia. The threat of drought is always a problem, but it becomes a much more severe threat as basic supplies of water around the world diminish and populations expand. Ethiopia's government is not perfect, but it is vastly improved from what it was a few years ago. An earlier harsh dictatorship had to appeal to the world for help during the region's severe drought more than a decade ago. Even the best possible government there must eventually cope with a population that is projected to grow from 54 million to approximately 122 million by the year 2025. How can Ethiopia sustain itself? Will it usurp the headwaters of the Nile and threaten the survival of other nations? And if the mushrooming population must be fed during a drought, how can even the wisest leaders handle the situation?

A century ago, 40 percent of Ethiopia had forest cover; now less than 4 percent is wooded. Farmers converted forests to cropland; animals killed vegetation by eating the leaves; and people desperate for fuel chopped down trees. All of this adds to Ethiopia's vulnerability.

Despite all of that, in Ethiopia and virtually every nation—developed and less developed—irrigation practices are tolerated that are wasteful of water. And with the poor practices comes erosion of topsoil, reducing future food production. Rivers are being polluted by fertilizers, pesticides, and untreated industrial waste, as well as raw sewage. Only a small percentage of Ethiopia's population has treated sewage. Open ditches carry most human waste, and as a result tens of thousands in the nation die each year from water-borne diseases.

Ethiopia is typical of many nations also in having rivers that run to and from other countries. Portions of Ethiopia are water-rich, but 90 percent of the water in Ethiopia comes from rivers that cross national boundaries. Ethiopia's leaders soon will face the dilemma of meeting either the water needs of their people or honoring their river commitments to other nations. And that dilemma will confront them even without a drought. Eighty-five percent of the Nile originates in Ethiopia, but the main beneficiaries of the Nile's waters under the current agreement are the Sudan and Egypt. The whole issue is so sensitive now that Ethiopia does not even share its water data with the other Nile nations.

Early in this decade, water scholar Joyce Starr convened an African summit on that subject. She pointed out in her opening remarks: "Worldwide, over 25,000 children are dying daily from hunger or disease caused by contaminated water or drought . . . most [of these deaths] occur in tropical Africa."[12] Those grim statistics are caused in part by the problem of every continent: The people are not necessarily where the water is. The Congo-Zaire basin has 50 percent of Africa's water but only 10 percent of the continent's people. When this book is published (in 1998), one-third of Africa's population will live in water-scarce areas and in less than thirty years that percentage will double—unless something happens to destroy much of the population or to address the international water crisis.

Unfortunately, shortages in nations everywhere are frequently combined with pollution problems. One small African example: Mwanza Town in Tanzania today has 420,000 people and is projected to have 1.2 million in fifteen years. Less than 15 percent of the population is hooked into sewers and the untreated wastes eventually flow into beautiful Lake Victoria. A 1994 World Bank report states: "Most of the industries of Mwanza do not have even simple treatment facilities. The main industries are textile manufacturing, cooking oil production, fish processing, leather tanning, printing works, soft drink production, garages, and oil jetties. All of them produce highly polluting wastes with high BOD5 [a general measure of pollution], and some release heavy metals in their effluent."[13] In the nation's capital, Dar-es-Salaam, leakage from water pipes is estimated between one-third and one-half of the flow.

Kenya has reached water shortages after years of plenty. The country now has a National Water Master Plan, but the Minister of Water Development complains that they do not have the financial resources to carry it out.

In South Africa, a White Paper issued by the Ministry of Water Affairs and Forestry sounds alarms for that nation's future. Twelve million of South Africa's 40 million people do not have safe water and 21 million lack basic sanitation—and it will get worse. The *Financial Mail* concluded: "The most frightening of the many statistics for the future South Africa are those related to water. . . . Without desalination or recycling, South Africa is likely to deplete available resources within the next fifteen years."[14]

The Western Sahara (formerly Spanish Morocco, or Spanish Sahara) remains in legal limbo, with a referendum on independence agreed to, in theory, by Morocco but again and again the election gets postponed. Western Sahara's appearance is as the name suggests: a vast desert area. Twenty years ago I spent a night in a tent in the desert, after visiting with the leaders of the independence movement there. I remember the enthusiasm of the people for independence, and the overwhelming sense I had of how-can-people-possibly-survive-here? As late as 1952 there were only twenty-four telephones in the entire territory, a piece of land larger than Great Britain. In 1959 that vast territory had six teachers. In 1960 the "country" had only 130 water wells.[15] Since 1960 the water prospects have improved with the development of deep wells that have tap aquifers and with some reliance on desalinated water. The water situation remains serious, however, and could get worse if the aquifers are depleted.

Also in northern Africa is Tunisia, which is plagued by shortages. Tunisia has one of the more sophisticated governments in all of Africa, but its leaders know that even with the maximum use of traditional sources for water, it faces severe problems. They are looking to nontraditional sources to rescue them. Tunisia is the only North African nation to have an integrated national plan for water.

Morocco, also in North Africa, has developed a somewhat less comprehensive plan, but Morocco cannot get around two realities: The water supply is declining and its population is rising. The decade that will soon end will see Morocco's population grow from 24 million to a projected 31 million.

One of the most exciting countries in Africa is Namibia, situated next to South Africa on the southern tip of the continent. It moved from colony status to independence only a decade ago, and many of those who opposed independence (in addition to the regime that then governed South Africa) feared that a harsh dictatorship would emerge. Instead, Namibia has a multiparty system and signs of a solid, mature government. A visitor is likely to be impressed by an official luncheon hosted by the nation's president to which he invites opposition party leaders. But Namibia faces major water problems that are restricting its development of arable land for food production. Worse yet, the groundwater sources are being depleted and irrigated land is suffering from salinization. Wood is used for fuel, as well as construction, and the deforestation brings desert problems. How much of this can a new democracy tolerate and still survive as a democracy? The director of the Department of Women's Affairs in Namibia, Nashilongo Elago Shivute, notes: "Namibian women are where American women were fifty years ago. Our priorities are different from those of the current American feminist movement. Women in America are shopping for dishwashers; women in the Third World are looking for water to wash the dishes."[16]

Sierra Leone in western Africa conducted a public survey of its environmental problems (including living conditions) and topping the list of a dozen citizen concerns are water contamination and water availability. That survey could have been conducted in more than 100 nations with similar results.

Bolivia in South America has adequate supplies of water but is one of the poorest nations in Latin America and has that region's lowest percentage of population served by piped water or a sewer system. Not surprisingly, Bolivia has a high rate of infant mortality, 75 per 1,000 births, and intestinal diseases are the second-leading cause of death in every age group. More than three-fourths of the people of Bolivia do not have piped water, and with more than 70 percent of the population living below the poverty line, the future for Bolivian citizens—particularly children—will remain bleak without assistance from other nations. Another South American nation, Chile, has huge mineral reserves in the northern part of the country, but potential expansion is sharply reduced by the lack of water.

My brother and his wife visited Georgetown, the capital of Guyana in South America. The people they visited had piped water, but it came out dark brown from the tap. Apparently the purification system is defective and the leaders of that nation cannot afford the needed improvements.

The developing nations face a good news/bad news situation in terms of providing water *quality* to their citizens. More people are being provided with piped water that may not be safe, but it is *safer.* The numbers not receiving piped water are also growing with the increasing population. *(When I speak about people receiving piped water, that ordinarily is not water piped into their home, but water piped into their neighborhood, where they can go and fetch it from relatively short distances.)*

At the end of the line for receiving safe water are the poor. They take what they can get, safe or unsafe, and as the supply of water at the end of the line diminishes, the quality of the water also decreases. The net result is less water for the poor, and more of the shrinking amount is contaminated. That means more disease, more premature deaths.

But don't imagine that developing nations, or Middle East nations, are the only areas troubled by water scarcity and pollution. The *London Financial Times* notes: "A recent report for the

European Commission argued that European growth could be constrained by a lack of freshwater caused by industrial and agricultural contamination."[17]

The Danube in central Europe is 1,700 miles long and runs through or affects water flow in seventeen nations. Amazingly, while there are difficulties, the nations have agreed on both water allocation and, more recently, on pollution reduction needs. A task force composed of representatives of twelve nations and seven international organizations monitors what is happening. It is an awkward administrative structure that could unravel at any time, but so far it appears to be working reasonably well. But as water becomes more precious, the possibility of conflicts rises.

Twenty-two countries around the world are dependent on the flow of water from other nations for a *majority* of their water, varying from Singapore (100 percent) to Turkmenistan (98 percent) to Germany (51 percent). In Africa there are fifty-seven river and lake basins that cross national boundaries. Portugal, with 48 percent of its water coming from outside its borders, does not fall into the top category of twenty-two nations receiving most of their water from other countries, but difficulties with Spain on water flow have caused the Food and Agriculture Organization in Rome to designate the Spanish-Portuguese frontier as "the most likely setting within Europe for an international clash over water resources."[18] The good news for Portugal is that it has fewer pollution problems than most of Europe. That does not remove its shortage, however, a problem the Portuguese government is starting to address more seriously. Poland, in contrast, is a water-surplus nation, but three-fourths of the water that flows in its rivers is too polluted for even primitive industrial use.

The drought in Spain of the early 1990s compounded all of that nation's supply difficulties. In the resort city of Fuengirola, for example, citizens had water available only on alternate days. Local citizens—not tourists—used mineral water for cooking and bathing. Spain anticipates as many as 8.5 million of its citizens facing serious water shortages soon.

Any visitor to Great Britain would have difficulty believing that England and Wales could have water problems! Yet there is heavy dependence on aquifers, and the National Rivers Authority, which has jurisdiction, is seriously concerned about growing pollution of groundwater.

Water-rich Canada would not appear to have any difficulties, other than some in the Saskatchewan region. Canada's rivers discharge 9 percent of the earth's renewable water supply. The United States (including Alaska), with seven times as much population as Canada, has rivers that discharge 8 percent. The International Joint Commission of Canada and the United States has more than 100 water conflicts pending before it, but because of the water wealth of Canada the public interest and concern have been minimal. However, a 1992 Canadian report reflects growing concern. It warned: "It is now apparent that many serious threats to the long-term sustainability of our own aquatic resources are directly linked to global circumstances."[19] The report notes increasing pollution of the ocean and declining fish stocks. It also observes that irrigation is increasing and points out the loss of 15 percent of irrigated land due to salinization. The report concludes that Canada's problem rests in large part on the fact "that we now consider our unsustainable use of aquatic resources as acceptable."[20]

Compounding problems for the future are national leaders who face overwhelming current difficulties, in countries like Uzbekistan and Turkmenistan in Central Asia, and who simply avoid facing the resource deficiencies of the years ahead.

A relatively smaller problem caused by water shortages is an actual physical drop in the level of the land, in limited areas, which is called subsidence. The United States has experienced a little of it, more often from coal mining than from water overuse. However, in scattered instances from Asia to Africa difficulties are developing—not a huge impediment for any nation, compared to water quantity and quality problems, but a cause for caution. Visitors to Mexico City have seen the grand Metropolitan Cathedral with a distinct tilt to parts of it. That is not caused by poor workmanship, but by the depletion of groundwater under the magnificent old church that caused the ground to sag. One of Mexico City's main roads now has a roller-coaster effect because of subsidence. In Xi'an, the capital of Shaanxi Province in China, the underground water table has dropped about 300 feet in forty years, and there is serious concern that further industrial and housing development could result in massive subsidence problems.

But land subsidence is a small difficulty on the horizon compared to the huge, looming water shortage, and the somewhat smaller but ominous problem of water quality deficiencies.

SECTION TWO

THE ANSWERS

7

DESALINATION

If we are heading toward a grave water crisis, which we are, and if 97 percent of the world's water is seawater, which it is, then one of the seemingly obvious answers to our looming catastrophe is to utilize seawater.

That answer is correct, but not simple.

The desalination technology is gradually, very gradually, moving ahead to the point that it is now becoming inexpensive enough for drinking water and household consumption. But more than 85 percent of the water that humanity uses is for agricultural and industrial purposes. Desalinated water is much too expensive for these uses, except in the oil-rich nations in the Middle East.

Seven years after he left the presidency, Dwight Eisenhower called for building four desalination plants in the Middle East to benefit both Israel and her Arab neighbors. Eisenhower wrote: "Most of the professional diplomats seem to think that we must have peace and stability in the Middle East before the plan can be implemented. I contend that the reverse is true: the proposal itself is a way to peace."[1] Senator Howard Baker of Tennessee introduced the Eisenhower proposal in the Senate, where it passed, but it died in the House. History will record that Eisenhower showed greater wisdom than the House. Seven years earlier, in his last State of the Union message to Congress, President Eisenhower called for "a farsighted . . . program for meeting urgent water needs . . . by converting saltwater to freshwater."[2]

The last bill of mine to pass Congress and be signed by President Clinton was a measure authorizing greater research to find less expensive ways of converting saltwater to freshwater. It passed the Senate with ease, as the Baker bill had, but got bogged down in the jurisdictional chaos of the House, where three committees had some technical involvement and jurisdiction. I called Speaker Newt Gingrich, who is open to new ideas, and explained the problem. He had two responses: "That's a bill that could save civilization," and then he added, "That's the idea Eisenhower promoted decades ago." Gingrich, to his credit, solved the jurisdictional problems, got the bill passed, and it went to the President's desk.

Eisenhower was not alone among presidents showing an interest in this process.

In 1790 the U.S. House of Representatives referred to Secretary of State Thomas Jefferson a petition from Jacob Isaacs of Rhode Island, who wanted to sell the federal government a means he had developed to convert saltwater to freshwater. Jefferson replied that Isaacs's system of distillation had been used on ships for thirty years, but he noted, the process is unknown "to the mass of seamen, to whom it would be the most useful."[3] Jefferson erred by a few years. In the fourth century B.C. Aristotle noted: "Saltwater, when it turns into vapor, becomes sweet and the vapor does not form saltwater again when it condenses."[4] In 1852 a British patent was granted for a desalination device, and nine years later the U.S. military purchased four of these devices.

At a press conference on April 12, 1961, a reporter asked President John F. Kennedy what scientific progress he would like to see in his administration. Kennedy replied: "We have made some exceptional scientific advances in the last decade, and some of them—they are not as spectacular as the man-in-space . . . but they are important. . . . If we could ever competitively, at a cheap rate, get freshwater from saltwater, that would be in the long-range interests of humanity [and] would dwarf any other scientific accomplishments. I am hopeful that we will intensify our efforts in that area."

Two months later in a speech, President Kennedy said: "I can think of no cause and no work which is more important, not only to the people of this country, but to people all around the globe. . . . I am hopeful that the United States will continue to exert great leadership in this field, and I want to assure the people of the world that we will make all the information that we have available to all people. We want to join . . . the scientists and engineers of other countries in their efforts to achieve one of the great scientific breakthroughs of history. . . . Before this decade is out we will see more and more evidence of man's ability at an economic rate to secure freshwater from saltwater, and when that day comes, then we will literally see the deserts bloom. This is a work . . . more important than any other scientific enterprise in which this country is now engaged. . . . It can do more to raise men and women from lives of poverty than any other scientific advance."[5]

In his presidential campaign of 1960, John Kennedy referred to the importance of this subject during speeches in at least eight states. In Billings, Montana, he said: "We will apply to the development of our resources the same scientific talents and energies which we have applied to the development of our national defense, inquiring into methods of . . . converting saltwater to freshwater, for whichever nation wins that race, to develop an economical way of using our seas for plant and human consumption, will have done more to win the friendship of people who live in deserts around great oceans than all the sputniks in outer space."[6]

For a period the United States pursued this initiative. But a recent Congressional Research Service report has these disheartening words: "Federal funding for most desalination research was discontinued in 1982."[7] In inflation-adjusted terms, the United States spent $144 million in desalination research in 1977, resulting in the only recent significant international scientific breakthrough, but twenty years later we are spending less than $2 million in this area—one-tenth of one percent as much as we spend on just one of the B-2 bombers that the Pentagon does not want and the Clinton administration did not request. The Defense Department has determined that it is unsafe to send the bomber overseas for missions, that its radar can't tell the difference between a rain cloud and a mountain, and that its skin "deteriorates in rain, heat, and humidity, requiring it to be extensively repaired each time it flies."[8] Congress voted for twenty-one of those bombers, yet our real, long-term security is tied infinitely more to desalination research than to building these ineffective weapons. U.S. naval ships have used desalinated water for decades, and in the recent conflict with Iraq, after its invasion of Kuwait, the United States relied on desalinated water for its land-based troops—water brought in from Saudi Arabia and the United Arab Emirates, as well as bottled water from Turkey.

Desalination research creates unexpected spinoffs that are of considerable consequence. A breakthrough in artificial kidney design occurred in 1967 with the hollow-fiber artificial kidney, marketed by Cordis Dow. It was based on a membrane developed by Henry Mahon and his coworkers at Dow Chemical to be used in desalination.[9]

The United States, which once led the world in desalination research, has abandoned that role now when it is most needed. The Saudis, the Israelis, and the Japanese are doing research, but no country other than the United States can galvanize a cooperative assault on the problem from all nations, and we're not doing it. Our country has adopted a policy of comfortable aloofness and indifference. Aside from the humanitarian and security interests the United States should have in desalination breakthroughs, there are also economic interests. When the United States led in desalination research, U.S. companies led in sales of desalination technology. Since abandoning that dominant role, others have moved into the manufacturing and sales leadership ahead of U.S. corporations. The manager for the Middle East and Africa for the Bechtel Corporation, a U.S. company with global projects, testified before a U.S. House committee and told Representative Tim Valentine, a North Carolina member who hoped for a desalination plant in his state, that fewer and fewer Americans and fewer and fewer companies in the United States are involved in desalination technology. The witness suggested the strong possibility that if North Carolina builds that plant in the next five years, it will be built by Japanese companies.[10] The United States once led in manufacturing and research of television and radio sets, but we largely abandoned both to others.

However, unlike the case with television and radio, the development of desalination is a life or death matter. "It is interesting for us to see the absence of U.S. leadership in these matters," a World Bank official tactfully told me.[11]

The United States headed research in this field until 1980, and then we bowed out. In 1977, for example, the United States led in research, sales, and manufacturing of desalination equipment. When we shut off our scientific inquiry, the Japanese and others bought much of our research and production. Two decades later Japan leads decisively in this field that will mushroom economically. Japan now produces and sells about three times as much desalination technology as the United States. Germany and Israel are also now major players. If this had happened because Japan invested much more than we did in research and plant capacity, that would be healthy for the world. The reality is that they moved ahead largely because the United States inexplicably abandoned the field. A look at the U.S. Patent Office gives an indication of how important the federal government's leadership can be. Between 1973 and 1986, that office registered eleven patents on desalination. Between 1986 and 1997 it registered one. In 1991 water specialist Joyce Starr wrote in *Foreign Policy*: "The U.S. government does not currently have the will to demonstrate significant global leadership on the water issue."[12] Matters have not changed substantially since then.

Not only is U.S. leadership lacking; sometimes it is *negative*. An official of the Bureau of Reclamation of the Department of the Interior testified before the Senate in 1995: "Because desalting technology is fairly well established, future Federal investment in this technology is questionable."[13] I could hardly believe I read those words from a responsible official. It is like suggesting that the development of the wheel makes any further investment in transportation technology questionable. His startlingly uninformed statement ignores need, technology, and almost everything that serious students of water now know. It should go down in history with the statement of the U.S. Commissioner of Patents in 1899: "Everything that can be invented has been invented."[14] The 1899 statement caused no harm. But government leaders who today utter this kind of nonsense threaten millions of lives. Contrast that statement with the 1971 enlightened testimony of Assistant Secretary of the Interior James Smith: "When we look at the projections of water consumption . . . and compare these projections with those for water availability, it becomes apparent that desalting technology will be a very important tool of water management."[15]

There are approximately 11,000 desalination plants in 120 nations in the world, 60 percent of them in the Middle East. The founder of modern Saudi Arabia ordered equipment for the first modern plant in 1938, although two small experimental plants had been built earlier in that nation, and there was one in Japan and one in Egypt. Three years ago Abu Dhabi in the United Arab Emirates in the Middle East boasted, with justification, that it had for the first time in world history a plant "producing 12 million gallons per day of distillate water with one desalination unit."[16] Others soon surpassed that claim to a notch in history. The cost of desalinated water is gradually coming down, and the cost of freshwater is gradually going up, but there remains a sizable gap between the two, and until that gap is closed, consumers understandably will continue to opt for the cheaper water. The desalting plants of the world now produce approximately 4 billion gallons of water daily, enough to provide every U.S. resident with fifteen gallons a day—but we are only slightly more than 4 percent of the world's population. Another way to understand where we are is that desalination plants provide about one-quarter

of 1 percent of the world's freshwater needs—better than nothing, but leaving a long way to go. A more positive way to look at
it is that desalination plants today are producing fifteen times as
much freshwater as they did twenty years ago. One plant in
Jidda, Saudi Arabia, produces 233 million gallons of water a day.

Although the United States is only starting to use desalting
techniques, we are one of the large users. The Middle East, as a
region, is by far the biggest participant, with Saudi Arabia leading all nations. Twenty-two of Africa's forty-seven nations now
have some form of small desalination facility. Desalting facilities
also operate in Cyprus, Malta, Gibraltar, the Caribbean, Cape
Verde, Portugal, Spain, Greece, Italy, India, China, Japan, and
Australia, for a total of 126 nations scattered across the globe.

In Cyprus the government is clear on where they must look for
survival: "The long-term prospect for a solution of the water
problem . . . is desalination of seawater."[17] Officials of Namibia in
Africa studied three potential sources for much-needed water:
importation from the interior, greater use of groundwater, and
desalination. Their tentative conclusion: desalination offers the
best answer. They have designed one plant and hope to model
others on it. Their big concern is the cost of energy.

Even in Antarctica there is a freshwater shortage. The U.S.
base on Ross Island has no unfrozen freshwater available. The
water they use from McMurdo Sound has to be desalinated.

Not only the needs are international, the answers are also. Countries exchange ideas and talent. Mekorot, the national Israeli
water corporation, is helping to build a unit in Spain. An Italian
firm helps Abu Dhabi. A Saudi company agreed to finance, own,
and operate a desalination plant in Egypt in the Hurgadah
region on the Red Sea, a spot with great tourism potential but little water. The Saudi company sells the desalinated water to

Egypt under a ten-year contract, a prototypical example of a privatization approach that is likely to expand. In theory, everyone should benefit. There are other examples. Few research and construction enterprises offer as many examples of international cooperation as the pioneering struggle on desalination.

.   .   .

What makes the use of saltwater so appealing is that most of the nations and areas with serious water shortages border the sea. And almost 70 percent of the world's population lives within fifty miles of the ocean.

Eighty-eight percent of California's population, for example, lives in coastal areas. A glance at the map of the U.S. East Coast shows the same; from Boston and New York down to Miami, huge concentrations of population are in coastal areas.

One other immense advantage of reliance on desalination of saltwater is that it is drought-free. California, the Midwest, Ethiopia, Central Europe, and almost every area of the world suffer from droughts periodically, and some are extremely costly. Even with heavy use of desalination, the effect on the ocean level is likely to be only marginal, if any. The greater danger we face is from rising ocean levels from greenhouse warming, discussed in the next part of this chapter. Having a drought-free source of water is already important, but if the scientists who participated in the United National Intergovernmental Panel on Climate Change are correct, then the gradually rising temperatures of the earth will cause ten times as many droughts annually by the year 2050.

In the United States, most of our desalting is done on brackish water in the interior of the country. Brackish water is water contaminated with higher than usable percentages of salt, and frequently other substances, but ordinarily is less saline than seawater. While most of the desalination in the United States is on brackish water, not seawater, the world picture is the opposite. Less than one-fourth of the earth's desalination plants work with brackish water, and the huge bulk of future desalination on the globe will use seawater. Desalting brackish water is less expensive than working with the higher salt content of ocean water. But it has drawbacks. First, disposal of the effluent from the desalting process in states like Nebraska and Colorado poses environmental problems. Second, as more and more of the brackish groundwater is brought to the surface, the salt content of the remaining water rises as the aquifer is depleted. Ocean desalination creates no environmental problems, as long as sensible procedures are followed. During the process, seawater is taken in and 30 to 50 percent is converted to freshwater. The balance of the seawater is returned to the ocean with approximately a double concentration of salt, but when it is returned, the ocean dilutes it immediately with no—or very slight—harmful effects. Additionally, the water is sent back to the ocean through a diffuser to avoid a sharp increase in salinity in any one spot.

The irony of this is that the United States spends money relatively freely for "innovative and cost-effective" projects like reducing interior salinity on the Colorado River, but devotes almost no money to research on desalinating seawater, which would provide far greater ultimate reward. In recent years the Bureau of Reclamation, the Bureau of Land Management, and the Department of Agriculture have spent almost $1 billion on interior salinity control measures, and only a tiny fraction of that amount on seawater desalination research and projects.

We do have desalting plants at the ocean's edge in several states, and each new plant that is built improves the process a little, as engineers learn how to more effectively deal with production problems. But the United States is crawling in the right direction when the world situation demands that we run.

.   .   .

How practical is desalination?

There are people who dismiss any substantial use of the oceans as a fantasy. Their philosophical relatives didn't believe in the steam engine or the cotton gin, electricity or air conditioning, radio or television. They are the modern-day equivalent of the Western Union official who sent an internal memorandum to other officers of the company in 1876: "This 'telephone' has too many shortcomings to be seriously considered as a means of communication. The device is inherently of no value to us."[18] Critics laughed at Leonardo da Vinci's plans for a flush toilet. We already are far beyond where many predicted desalination could go. *If we spent 5 percent as much each year on desalination research as we spend on weapons research, in a short time we could enrich the lives of all humanity far beyond anything anyone has conceived.*

This fiscal year (1998) Congress appropriated approximately $37.9 billion for military research. Five percent of that would be $1.9 billion. Such an expenditure for desalination research could have staggering results for a better world. And the United States, which once led the world in manufacturing desalination equipment, could emerge as the leader again in a market with huge potential. Finding a markedly less expensive method of converting saltwater to freshwater would alleviate the problems of most of the world's water-poor areas.

The two basic processes in use now are distillation and reverse osmosis. By far the most widely used is distillation—the basic process that nature now utilizes when it takes water vapor from the ocean through the sun's rays and then returns it to the earth as snow and rain. Reverse osmosis, the primary process in the United States, is a system that uses membranes to reject the salt. Through research, improvements on both processes—or some new process—may be found, and there are more than a handful of inventors who have such ideas. What is clear is that the most cursory look at where we are today indicates there is a huge potential for improvement. Now, with the 1996 desalination research measure that President Clinton signed, there is hope for that improvement. But strictly in dollars appropriated, we are a long distance from where we once were and where the needs dictate we should be.

Other nations are slowly and partially filling the vacuum left by the United States, including a Middle East desalination research center in Oman. The United States is committed to eventually provide $3 million for the center, and besides Israel and the Arab countries, other nations indicating they will participate include Japan, South Korea, and the European Union. But as in so many areas, U.S. leadership is vital—and lacking. This is partially offset by investments in research by major corporations that have accounted for some of our progress. The American Water Works Association Research Foundation has the potential to contribute significantly also.

.　　　.　　　.

What should add some sense of urgency to the need for action is the warming that is taking place on the earth. It is called the "greenhouse warming," because the warming process that is occurring works like one. In a greenhouse, the glass panels let light and heat in but trap them inside. The layer of gases that go into the atmosphere from industrial pollutants work the same way, letting the heat in but trapping it near the earth's surface. A look at global average temperatures from 1860 to 1990 shows variation but a clear, slow trend toward higher temperatures. Those who claim there is no earth warming, particularly the major oil companies, cite anecdotal evidence and, in all fairness, sometimes the supporters of the global warming theory do the same. But in addition to the actual trend toward higher temperatures, watching Antarctica may be a particularly effective way to gauge the future. Temperatures there have risen almost twenty degrees Fahrenheit in the last twenty years.[19] And in 1995 a shelf of ice larger than Rhode Island broke off the ice mass there. Four of the earth's warmest years since 1866 have occurred in the 1990s. There is general agreement that the principal cause of this is the increase in chemicals, particularly chlorofluorocarbons (CFCs), which we use for refrigeration and things as widely used as hairsprays.

Vice President Al Gore has an excellent discussion of global warming in his book *Earth in the Balance*. Scientists are not in agreement on what the full impact of it will be. However, virtually all scientists who have studied this phenomenon conclude that the increase of greenhouse gases in the atmosphere and the thinning of the ozone layer, which helps shield the earth from excessive heat from the sun, (1) are harming humanity with more skin cancer, (2) will multiply droughts, and (3) will cause the ocean level to rise as more and more snow and ice melt. Some predictions of ocean rise are as low as a few inches, but most forecast a greater increase. The 1992 study by the National Academy of Sciences and two other groups concludes that *in the absence of preventive action*, the sea may rise from zero to twenty-four inches by the end of the next century. Who is right? I do not know. No one does. But prudence dictates that we do what we can to protect the earth and reduce the impact of a rising ocean. It is difficult to disagree with the conclusion of Jessica Matthews: "Global warming is . . . an international security issue with stupendous economic and ecological stakes."[20]

And human stakes. Ponder these words: "Melanoma [skin cancer] deaths are up fivefold over the past fifty years in Australia, up eighty-three percent over the past seven years in the U.S., and increasing three to seven percent a year worldwide."[21] Are we certain these statistics are caused by the greenhouse effect and the related thinning of the ozone layer? No. Does it seem probable? Yes.

Prime Minister Tony Blair of Great Britain is a strong friend of the United States and a personal friend of Bill Clinton. Nevertheless, he is sharply critical of the United States for not taking the global warming threats more seriously. At the world summit in Rio de Janeiro the United States said we would lead the charge to avoid further warming of the earth. We haven't.

A heading of an article in the *New York Times* (October 21, 1997) unfortunately tells much of the story: "U.S. Emits Greenhouse Gases at the Highest Rate in Years." The report says:

As negotiations resume in Bonn on a new treaty to save the planet from global warming, the United States said today that its emissions of heat-trapping gases into the atmosphere grew last year at the highest rate since the nation pledged to cut them back. . . .

The report is acutely embarrassing to American negotiators at the climate talks, because the United States, with less than a twentieth of the world's population, gives almost a fourth of the gases that trap heat in the atmosphere, threatening widespread climate change.

In a treaty on climate change signed by 160 nations in 1992, the United States and other industrial countries pledged to reduce their emissions of such gases to 1990's level by 2000.

But American emissions in 1996 were 7.4 percent above 1990 levels, the report said. . . . By the end of the decade, emissions of the gases in the United States will be 13 percent higher than in 1990.[22]

This U.S. half-heartedness in dealing with this threat could result in serious damage to states like Florida and much of the world.

Every inch the ocean rises means greater penetration of salt into inland aquifers. For residences and businesses on the ocean's edge, it means increased danger from the rising water and from high winds that stir the water. If the ocean rises one foot, the entire coast of Florida is in serious trouble.

What can be done about the greenhouse effect? Five steps, at least, should be taken quickly:

1. Reduce, and eventually eliminate, the use of chloro-fluorocarbons (CFCs).

This product, for which there generally are substitutes, is found in air-conditioning systems, refrigerators, and aerosol cans.

The scientific community agrees that CFCs damage the ozone and we can do well without them. In 1987 thirty-one nations met in Canada and signed an accord to cut the emissions of CFCs by half. Since then, 139 nations have signed the protocol. The United States led the way on this, as it must in many areas if the community of nations is to act in concert. The aim is to reduce CFC use by 45 percent by the year 2009, but developing nations don't like to turn their backs on tools that will improve their standard of living, and even the United States has not been as enthusiastic as it should be about taking this relatively small step by which it and other industrial nations can markedly reduce ozone depletion.

Are small steps important? Scientists at Utrecht University in the Netherlands believe that the steps already taken are *reducing the growth* of the number of people with skin cancer caused by the depleted ozone. They suggest that as many as 1.5 million skin cancers have been avoided in the United States alone by actions taken to implement this recommendation and the next (number 2 below). While CFCs are not a large part of the greenhouse gases, they do contribute to the whole, and because they also reduce the ozone layer that protects the earth from the sun, they are a contributing factor of some significance to global warming.

2. Take steps to reduce carbon dioxide and sulfur dioxide emissions.

On a per capita basis, the United States is far and away the world's greatest carbon dioxide and sulfur dioxide polluter. Prior to the unification of Germany, East Germany had a worse record than we have, but now we stand in lonely eminence. On a per capita basis our carbon dioxide emission, for example, is eighteen times that of India. But nations from China to the Czech Republic also contribute. Utility plants emit about one-third of the global total of carbon dioxide and an even higher percentage of sulfur dioxide. Those figures are significant because, with the projected doubling of the world's population in the next five or six decades, the general assumption is that the world standard of living also will gradually rise. That could mean not a doubling of demands for electricity, but more likely a tripling. Can utilities provide this assistance to us without adding to the carbon dioxide and sulfur dioxide problems? Giving utilities tax credits for installing scrubbers at their plants would greatly reduce part of the problem and would do it quickly. Carbon dioxide is the principal contributor to greenhouse gases. Sulfur dioxide is primarily associated with acid rain. But a joint assault on both, through the utilities, would benefit our nation and all humanity.

Some increase in the U.S. gasoline tax could help the nation and the world by encouraging greater use of gasoline-efficient cars. This would reduce our carbon dioxide emissions. But we are avoiding these simple solutions in the ill-directed zeal of political leaders who pander to the public by outbidding one another with promises of no tax increases, or even tax decreases. Even after a highly publicized White House meeting on global warming and discussion of the urgent need to reduce carbon dioxide, President Clinton ruled out the one action that could bring quick results: a gasoline tax increase. Jeanne and I recently took a ten-day vacation, flew to Madrid, and rented a car and drove around Spain and Portugal. Their "interstate" roads are in much better shape than ours—but we paid $4.50 a gallon for gasoline. No major nation in the world has lower gasoline taxes, except Saudi Arabia. Each penny of gas tax produces $1.2 billion. If the United States were to take even the modest step of increasing gasoline taxes eight cents a gallon—using one cent for Amtrak and its beleaguered passenger rail service, two cents for state and local roads, two cents for interstate highways, two cents for mass transit, and one cent for research on electric cars—these forms of transportation would be measurably improved. It would be a modest step to improve our economy and a small step toward reducing our carbon dioxide emissions. I favor a gasoline tax increase much greater than eight cents, but that is not doable politically without courageous leadership.

One not-so-incidental by-product of high sulfur dioxide emissions is that they reduce the protein level of grass on which cattle feed. Precisely why this is so is not entirely clear. But the sulfur dioxide emission results in requiring cattle to eat more grass, and in the process consume more water, to achieve a pound of high protein.

Combining creativity and common sense can save energy and reduce pollution. The new headquarters in Amsterdam of the large Internationale Nederlanden Bank uses 10 percent as much energy as the old office. It saves money and energy.

3. We need much greater research on utilization of solar power.

Leon Awerbuch of the Bechtel Corporation, one of the far-sighted leaders on desalination, writes: "In the long run, sustainable [desalination] development requires us to look at renewable sources like solar energy and its derivatives, wind, ocean thermal, waves, and alternative energy like nuclear, because of limits of supply of fossil fuel and the potential impact of [the] greenhouse effect."[23]

Of the more than 10,000 desalination plants now in existence—almost all in sun-baked areas—only seventy use solar power for energy. One of the nation's most thoughtful and balanced environmental writers, Gregg Easterbrook, believes that "solar power and wind power, disappointments in the past, appear to be on the verge of a takeoff."[24] That may sound like a replay of what we heard during the 1970s energy crunch, but there is substantial activity to back his claim. In at least a score of nations, there are significant developments in wind and solar energy. Denmark now supplies 3 percent of its electricity through wind turbines. The potential of solar power can be seen in Israel on the road from the Tel Aviv airport to the city. Soon after leaving the airport and joining the multilane highway from Jerusalem to Tel Aviv, the visitor encounters hundreds of relatively new apartment buildings, all with solar devices to heat water, which takes about 20 percent of the energy in a nonsolar household.

Solar research is particularly significant for desalination because the areas that have water problems generally have an abundance of sun. One of the difficulties that still needs to be addressed is that so much area is needed to create significant amounts of solar energy, but in Florida, Greece, Portugal, Japan, and Israel there are experiments with different processes that use little more space than conventional power plants. Placing barges offshore with solar collectors is also being studied. Pacific Gas and Electric in California is using wind power, an offshoot of solar, for a small part of its energy. The Luz Corporation of Israel is developing solar energy plants for Southern California Edison Company.

The conventional type of solar collector—if anything about solar energy can be called conventional—is the type of collector you see on a home. Solar ponds are an alternative in the experimental stage. Ponds are literally bodies of water that collect solar energy and also provide long-term heat storage, an ability the other collectors do not have. They are also less expensive to construct.

Solar and other possible energy sources are also needed to avoid the harm that we are doing to our atmosphere, and our future, through excessive emission of carbon dioxide and sulfur dioxide, the major polluting factors of the more conventional energy sources. The Weizmann Institute in Israel is doing research on the prospects of collecting solar power and shipping it by "solar energy pipeline" to customers in Israel and other countries.[25] While I doubt that solar cars will be part of our future, there have been races in the United States with cars powered by solar energy. Electric cars are much more likely, a not-so-incidental gain because it takes fifty gallons of water to produce one gallon of gasoline.

Solar photovoltaic cells, called PVs, are small solar conversion devices that permit operating everything from a lamp to a television set. The Japanese have perfected it to the point that they sell about 100 million a year, mostly in developing nations, but Idaho Power Company installs and maintains small units in the mountainous portions of northern Idaho that are not reached by electric lines. This is not a substitute for a grid system that should eventually bring electricity to all homes on the earth, but it demonstrates the potential of solar power. And that includes economic potential. In June 1996, the front page of the business section of the *New York Times* ran a heading: "U.S. Solar Industry in Export Boom."[26] "Boomlet" might have been a better word. It is still a small industry, whose actions do not even cause a ripple on our economic scene, but it is growing and will continue to do so.

My home in southern Illinois is passive solar, built to take advantage of the sun's rays, and during the coldest days of winter, when the sun is shining, our furnace does not kick on except at night. (I asked the architect who planned our home what was the thickest insulation available. When he told me, I said to him, "Double it.") We save energy, we save money.

Not all of these developments are monumental breakthroughs, but they indicate the potential of solar energy, and with even small investments in research, the sun could power much more and we would not need to pollute our atmosphere as much. Solar energy is now growing more rapidly in other nations than it is in the United States.

Using solar power as the energy source for desalination ultimately makes a great deal of sense, but the limited research on this, up to now, has been only marginally successful. A gradually growing number of authorities are in agreement with the conclusion of three scientists from the United Arab Emirates: "Solar energy conversion systems are one of the most promising of the renewable energy sources of the Gulf countries."[27] No less an authority than the chief executive officer of Shell Oil in Great Britain, a branch of the Dutch corporation, the world's most profitable oil company, says that hydro power and nuclear energy will fill part of the void as fossil fuels decline, but that solar energy and wind energy (classified as part of solar) will be "far more important."[28] Putting substantial resource dollars into solar energy research is an obvious need that will have long-term payoffs.

Research on cleaner and less dangerous methods of utilizing nuclear energy also should be pursued. I have never been an enthusiast for the use of nuclear energy as it is now being produced, but fusion and other nuclear alternatives need study. Environmentally safer nuclear energy is within reach, if research is pushed, and while nuclear energy presently creates other problems, it does not contribute to the buildup of greenhouse gases. Theoretically, the use of nuclear energy could reduce global warming by as much as 30 percent.

The automobile is the big carbon dioxide culprit. Peugeot now sells an electric motor scooter. General Motors will soon produce a semi-experimental electric car. Most electric cars have been based on battery power, with the research aimed at improving battery performance. Ford Motor Company is joining with a German automobile manufacturer to develop electric cars run by fuel cells that operate on a combination of hydrogen and oxygen, and whose only emission is water.

Another recent development, apparently of some substance, has resulted in designing an electric car that is not battery powered, but uses about one-tenth of the gasoline of current automobile models. Developed by Arthur D. Little Inc., the new electric car would reduce pollution by 90 percent. Secretary of Energy Frederico Pena said it is "a terrific breakthrough," but adds the disquieting news that the cars cannot be manufactured for public sale until 2010. It is hard to believe that if we have the basic technology, that perfecting it must take us until the year 2010—if we believe it is a high priority. Chrysler is now showing a keen interest in this new technology and that may hasten its development and sales. Delving into the potential of electric automobiles has met with resistance from the oil industry, for obvious reasons, but breakthroughs—not far off now—will come if we promote studies more aggressively. Our environment will thank us if we do it.

4. Plant trees. Millions of them. Billions of them. Perhaps trillions of them.

If the United Nations by resolution were to call on every nation to plant one tree per person each year for the next five years, it would have the following results ten and twenty years from now: beautify our earth; improve air quality; reduce the encroachment of the desert; reduce flooding; protect and renew the topsoil; protect wildlife; provide fuel for those who use wood for that purpose; provide construction materials; and, of no small significance, stabilize water resources and reduce the flow of water to the sea.

Dwayne Andreas, the visionary leader of Archer Daniels Midland Corporation, calls for a loftier goal than I have set. "We need to plant trillions of trees," he says. "A grove of trees holds up as much water as a lake. We need hedgerows as windbreaks."[29] But even if we scale down his request, and I favor his idea, each year planting one tree per person on the earth, 5.7 billion trees, that would be an immense contribution to humanity.

For the United States, that would mean 250 million trees annually. That should not be difficult to attain. For some people in central cities who cannot easily plant a tree, some of the rest of us could plant two, or ten, or twenty. As I sit at my typewriter working on this book, I can look out my window and see a tree I planted about ten years ago that is now more than sixty feet tall. It took only a few minutes to plant it.

Each year, more than 37 million acres of tropical forests are lost, either for acreage for farmers or for lumber, or both. Within the United States and other developed nations, wooded areas often give way for the same purposes, as well as housing developments, parking lots, and shopping malls.

China has reforested some areas. It could and should do much more, but it has done better than almost all nations. An Agency for International Development project had Haiti's farmers planting 250 trees a year per aid recipient. Private voluntary organizations like CARE have helped with this. In 1983 the state of Gujarat in India planted ten trees for each citizen there. If Gujarat's leaders can take action to plant ten trees per person, it is not asking too much for the rest of the world to plant one tree per person. Two decades ago South Korea provided three *billion* seedlings for its citizens to plant. How many of those actually were planted no one knows, but if even one-tenth were planted, that would be 300 million trees. Adding some sense of urgency to this is the gradual—in some cases rapid—destruction of the tropical rain forests for short-term gains that will result in major long-term losses for all of humanity. Madagascar, as one illustration, is losing 250,000 acres of forest every year. Environmental writer Gregg Easterbrook provides encouragement to all of us, pointing out that when steps are taken to *re*forest areas, it can happen. Maine, for example, once had 74 percent of its land in woods. Now it is 90 percent. Modest steps like simply planting more trees can make a huge difference for the future of humanity.

5. Push research on desalination much more aggressively.

If scientists search to find less expensive ways of converting saltwater to freshwater, desert areas all over the world can bloom with trees and the plants of food production. The combination of growing trees and using saltwater from the seas, when added to efforts to reduce greenhouse gases and the threat to the ozone layer, can reduce ocean levels rather than allow them to rise, or at the very least, diminish the amount of rise of the oceans.[30] Reducing the ocean level, or its rise, by even one inch can have a huge impact in safeguarding inland ground aquifers from salt invasion.

If a significant greenhouse warming does take place, not only will the oceans rise but sources of freshwater will decline. For example, California's transfer of water from the northern part of that state to the south would decrease because of diminished snows in the north. Similar factors around the globe add to the importance of urgently moving ahead on desalination research. But we have no sense of urgency. The United States now has an Interagency

Consortium for Desalination and Membrane Separation Research. Distillation, the most commonly used form of desalination on the earth, is not even mentioned in its latest report. How often do they meet? Once a year. In 1996 the executive director of the Interstate Council on Water Policy wrote to me complaining about "the inflexibility of federal water policies."[31] The problem is not only inflexibility. It is the lack of vision, the need for a dream, some comprehension of the nature of the world we will soon face, and an urgent commitment to do something about it.

The head of the World Meteorological Organization says: "The global warming to which we are already committed is irreversible. . . . By the time we detect it, it will be too late."[32] *He may be right; he may be partially wrong.* At least, we should mitigate the potential catastrophe by acting quickly and sensibly. Former senator George Mitchell, a leader on environmental issues, put it this way: "The issue is not stopping the world from warming at all. That isn't now possible. Some warming has been locked in. The challenge now is to slow the production of the greenhouse gases as soon as possible, to slow future warming, to avoid the most sudden and catastrophic climate changes."[33] And somewhat encouraging is the National Academy of Sciences report that carbon dioxide stays in the atmosphere "for decades, at least" when the assumption had been made that it would last for centuries.[34] But that news is encouraging only if we act decisively and quickly. Their report suggests it is *possible* to avoid the most devastating effects, if we show wisdom and courage and speed. Carbon dioxide could gradually become less of a threat—but that is not even a possibility unless the world's leaders act, and the United States in particular must lead.

.　　.　　.

Avishay Braverman, the impressive president of Ben-Gurion University of the Negev, headed a study for the World Bank on the future of water in the Middle East. Its conclusion: the only long-term answer is desalination of seawater. He says that sizable quantities of desalinated water will be needed by 2010. He notes that getting water from the sea reduces or eliminates the multinational problems and he stresses two other basics: "A downward trend is foreseen in the cost of erecting new water desalination projects and maintaining those presently operating, due to technological improvements expected in the next twenty years. And seawater is the only existing quantitatively unlimited source of water."[35] Shimon Peres's book, *The New Middle East*, is filled with references to the need for desalination research. He calls for a breakthrough in that quest. Peres writes: "The Middle East is a pioneer in this area on a global scale: at the end of the previous decade [1990], close to 5 billion cubic millimeters of water were desalinated annually worldwide, with half [of that] in the Middle East, especially in Saudi Arabia, Kuwait, and the Gulf principalities. Eilat and Aqaba have desalination facilities to meet the needs of their residents. The oil-producing countries can desalinate water on a large scale; they have no freshwater sources, and for them the oil required for desalination is cheaper than water. Therefore, desalination in some Middle Eastern areas is economically viable, but this is not yet true in Israel, Jordan, Syria, and Egypt. . . . The sum total of desalinated water worldwide is equal to the water Egypt consumes in one month."[36]

The improved relationship between Israel and Jordan has renewed talk about a canal from the Red Sea to the Dead Sea, helping to supply potentially 850 million cubic meters per year of freshwater through desalination to both countries. Because the Dead Sea is the lowest point on earth, over 1300 feet below sea level, a reverse osmosis desalination plant could operate without electrical energy, the energy being driven by hydrostatic devices. The effluent from the desalination plant would still be appreciably less salty than the Dead Sea, which is approximately six times saltier than the Mediterranean. It would also resurrect the steadily declining level of the Dead Sea. There still may be environmental and economic questions about the wisdom of such a canal, but until recently the barrier has been political. That barrier appears to be diminishing. The freshwater would have to be pumped to the higher elevations of Amman, Jerusalem, and Jericho, but would be a major assist to meeting their future water needs. It would be a multibillion-dollar undertaking, but offers an integrated approach to development. A recent study by the Bechtel Corporation projected significant economies from the project, a unique solution to part of the critical water needs of that area.

The late Prime Minister Yitzhak Rabin said: "Israel will be like a Garden of Eden again if we can get water inexpensively from the Mediterranean."[37] When Rabin and King Hussein of Jordan spoke to a Joint Session of Congress in 1994, a small luncheon honored the two leaders afterward. At the head table they sat on either side of Vice President Al Gore. I went to pay my respects to the two of them, and the Vice President told me, "They've just been lobbying me for your bill on desalination research."

A study supported by the U.S. Institute for Peace, published in the *Natural Resources Journal,* suggests that "large-scale regional desalination projects" in the Middle East could both meet the serious water demands and foster greater cooperation between the nations of that region.[38] World Bank officials told me, "The only solution for the Gaza Strip is desalination."

There are more than forty large desalination plants in the

Middle East, thirty-four of them in Saudi Arabia. The Saudis must rely on desalination more and more. Between 1985 and 1990 the government there spent more than $8.5 billion on desalination water projects, far more than any other nation. Demand for water in Saudi Arabia has more than doubled in the last two decades, and by the end of the century, desalination plants will supply over 800 million gallons a day. That is a great deal of water but small compared to global use. It is three times what Las Vegas uses, twelve times what Tampa uses, fifty times more than Springfield, Illinois, uses, but only four-fifths of what Chicago uses. Saudi Arabia is now piping desalinated water over long distances, and more pipelines are planned. The Saudis have abundant oil supplies for energy, easing their glide into desalination, but oil and non-oil nations in the region are moving toward more and more desalination. At the university in Jidda, the Saudis established a Department of Thermal Engineering and Desalination Technology. (The University of Glasgow in Scotland also has a program. A University of California curriculum that includes desalination is the closest U.S. comparison.) But there is an unanswered question in the Saudi situation: Will this growing water resource be overtaken by their population explosion?

The Sultan of Oman, interviewed in April 1995, said: "With our long coastline, if the need arose, further desalination plants could be established."[39] The need will arise! Kuwaiti officials claim that "no other country on earth is so totally dependent upon desalination technologies."[40] One or two nations might contest that claim; more will soon, particularly in the Middle East. While the use of oil to provide energy for desalination is sensible at the moment for most countries in that region, it does not make sense yet for most of the world, certainly not for producing water for agricultural and industrial needs. Egypt has joined four other North African nations requesting a study on the possible use of nuclear energy for desalination. But even if nuclear energy is not used, one study for Egypt concludes that its "arid coastal regions on both the Mediterranean and Red Sea have excellent [sites] for future [desalination] development."[41] Almost the same could be said of most of the Middle East and North African countries.

Israel has been using desalination technology for brackish water purification, but recognizes the progress in seawater desalination research and is moving more and more toward seawater desalination. The head of engineering for the national Israeli water company, Mekorot, wrote to me: "I believe that there is no way to avoid seawater desalination in large scale in the future."

Illustrating what is happening in desalination technology is the Sabha plant in Israel. *In 1978, the process recovered (purified) 49 percent of the water intake, but by 1994, that reached 70 percent. And the energy to produce the 70 percent is almost half what it took to produce the 49 percent.* Into all equations must be added the balancing factor of large population growth. But desalination is the brightest distant light in an otherwise dark picture.

The Middle East is also illustrative of most of the water-poor areas of the world in one important respect: It has an abundance of the sun's rays and great solar energy potential. But until solar is more fully developed, traditional sources for energy must be used. Building desalination plants next to utility facilities will happen more and more, utilizing the wasted energy of such a plant. A slight modification of that is being seriously discussed: to use energy from utility plants for desalination in their off-peak hours. For example, most of the time utilities run at 30 to 40 percent of capacity. Storing the balance of that electricity for future use is technically not feasible. But storage of water is simple. If during the off-peak hours utilities were to be used to generate freshwater from saltwater, there would be substantial gains at relatively low costs.

California leads most states in having serious water problems, but California is also ahead of most states in what will become an increasingly important part of our national and international solution: desalination of seawater. On new supply, the Pacific Institute reports, "One possibility stands out . . . the use of saltwater desalination when that desalination is accompanied with renewable energy."[42]

California has nineteen desalination plants either operating or under construction. A few, like the one at Oceanside, are expanding. I visited two of California's desalination plants. One is on Catalina Island, where Southern California Edison opened a small one (132,000 gallons per day). But every new desalination plant is significant because with almost every new facility, some bit of knowledge is developed that will make the next one constructed more efficient, more productive. More important than the exceptionally good company at Catalina was the attitude of enthusiasm there on the part of the utility executives. They gradually came to see the process as important to their business and to civilization.

California, not surprisingly, has the largest water district in the nation, the Metropolitan Water District of Southern California, which serves sixteen million people. Fortunately, the district's leaders understand the immensity of the problems they will face. They have a small demonstration desalination plant in Huntington Beach that produces 2,000 gallons of freshwater a day; they are moving toward a much larger plant that will give them five million gallons a day. More important than the amount is that the plant will use a somewhat different process of distillation, which represents a developmental breakthrough.

Of more than casual interest to Americans should be the fact that a California metropolitan water district is receiving foreign aid from Israel of $2 million for this development—while our own government is making only token efforts in the direction of desalination research.

This California experiment is trying everything from different pipes to deal with saltwater corrosion, to minor technical changes, any of which could ultimately be important. There are now, as this book is being written, at least six serious but small research endeavors under way around the world, any one of which *could* make a dramatic breakthrough. The more likely scenario is that the differing inventions and procedures will each make relatively small, incremental improvements. If in addition to these six (and others that I do not have knowledge of), if there were fifty or a hundred creative idea people working on possibilities, progress on this urgent matter would be significantly enhanced. That is not likely to happen without leadership from the U.S. government.

The metropolitan water district has this fascinating cost summary for its experiment: "The cost for potable water from currently operating seawater desalination plants around the world ranges from $2,000 to $6,000 per acre-foot [326,000 gallons]. Estimates for water produced from new, but not yet built, seawater desalination plants range from $1,100 through $1,600 per acre-foot."[43] One estimate given to the *Los Angeles Times* for the new California plant is that it may have production and refinement costs as low as $850 per acre-foot. That compares with costs from freshwater sources for the district of $412 to $800 per acre-foot. Two things are significant: One, the cost of the conventional sources for water is gradually rising, and two, the cost of freshwater from seawater is gradually declining. Advances in solar energy technology could accelerate the closing of the price gap between the two processes.

Declining cost is not the only reason California is looking with yearning at desalinated water. In 1995 a witness for the Metropolitan Water District of Southern California told a U.S. House subcommittee that desalted water is appealing because it is "a new source of highly pure supplemental water that is not subject to droughts or earthquakes"—the latter of growing importance to California.[44] When he speaks of "a highly pure supplemental water," desalinated water from the ocean is precisely that. It is purer than almost any other source of water. Snow is generally purer than rainwater, and desalinated water from the distillation process is purer than snow. Reverse osmosis produces desalinated water that exceeds the standards for drinking water, though it is not as pure as distilled water. Limited medical studies on desalinated water are overwhelmingly positive, including a substantial reduction in kidney problems for those who use the desalinated product. One study suggests that drinking desalinated water may contribute to loss of hair, but that can be countered by the use of hair oil and protein-rich shampoo.[45] The demand for purer water is growing, even at the industrial level. U.S. and foreign industries requiring purer water include electronics, semiconductor, pharmaceutical, medical, food and beverage.

The Key West, Florida, desalination facility and the Morro Bay, Santa Barbara, and Catalina Island plants in California operate primarily on a standby basis because of the cost of the desalination process, which limits its use. Santa Barbara's is the most recent to be built and go on standby status. Municipal authorities authorized its construction during the period of severe water shortage, 1988 to 1992. It is there now as a supplement, a vital water source that is available when the more conventional and less expensive sources are inadequate. The day will come when the citizens of Santa Barbara will be grateful for this. In the meantime, all of us can be grateful. Again, each time a new plant is built, we increase our knowledge of how to do the job better.

· · ·

Since 1992, Patricia Mulroy, general manager of the Southern Nevada Water Authority, has been exploring the possibility of Nevada helping California develop desalination, and in return, getting some of California's share of the Colorado River. While such an arrangement would be complicated—everything about water is complicated—it looks like the most sensible long-term solution to Nevada's difficulties. That possibility becomes more of a likelihood as scientific inquiry reduces the cost of desalination.

Whatever helps California, Texas, or Florida also helps inland areas. To the extent that Texas and California, for example, can successfully utilize desalination, that should relieve excessive use of aquifers, protecting the groundwater in the process, but also assisting neighboring states because aquifers do not follow state lines. And all the Colorado River states will be aided if California can become less dependent on that river. It is also likely that eventually water will be piped from the sea to some inland areas. Pumping water from the ocean to Phoenix, for example, would add only about 20 percent to the cost of water delivered to that Arizona community.[46]

Florida delegates all authority over water to five regional water management districts. A 1995 study by the Southwest

Florida Water Management District came to this conclusion: "Seawater desalination holds great potential to meet the current and future needs for Tampa Bay."[47] In cooperation with others, including the Florida Department of Environmental Protection, the district also did a careful study of the environmental impact of removing salt from the ocean and concluded that the research "has demonstrated that seawater desalination can be a safe, dependable and environmentally-compatible water supply source."[48] A Sarasota newspaper heading tells the story: "Clock Is Ticking in Search for Water." The subhead reads: "Many Experts Believe the Answer Is to Remove the Salt from Gulf Waters."[49] Florida already has more than 130 desalination plants, but they are all small and account for only a tiny fraction of Florida's freshwater usage.

Some Florida officials talk about desalination coming in a major way by the year 2030, but others acknowledge that time period will have to be shortened. Peter Gottschalk, cochair of the Coalition of Lake Associations in Florida, says, "Desalination needs to become an increasing supply of water [soon]. I'd rather see the ocean desalinated than water sucked out from under my property."[50] A key water official in that state observes: "Florida is giving seawater desalination serious consideration as a long-term, dependable water supply source. . . . Our environment is being seriously compromised by traditional ground and surface water withdrawals."[51]

The danger for Florida and other states and countries is that by the time a real crisis is imminent it will be too late to move effectively on desalination without having a considerable time gap that will be expensive both in dollars and humanitarian terms. Building before technology is further perfected can be expensive, but waiting too long can be far more expensive.

Part of the Texas Water Plan, submitted by that state's Water

Development Board, is that the Texas legislature should support national efforts to promote desalination. While "promoting" desalination is welcomed, what will really promote it is research that gets the cost down. A subsequent supplemental report is more specific and urges water research by the Lone Star State's universities. An indication of things to come is a small item in a bulletin: "Desalination success stories from projects around Texas are forming the foundation for an increasing demand for desalinated water."[52] Waiting for a sure thing will not solve the desalination problem any more than it brought us the cure for polio.

An example of the kinds of improvements that can change the picture is an invention developed by National Advanced Technology Exchange of Woodland Hills, California. It uses the membranes of the reverse osmosis process but appears to reduce energy costs dramatically. An outside engineering firm has made a favorable analysis. Dennis Chancellor, the chief executive officer of the California developers, explained the process to me in some detail. Since I don't have the technical expertise to evaluate the process, I referred it to a specialist who gave it a guarded green light, indicating that it appeared to have real potential. This type of idea deserves to have a careful evaluation, and if that evaluation is favorable, then a demonstration unit to actually produce freshwater should be built. We must be willing to try and fail, or we will never achieve the breakthroughs needed. Ventures Plus, a Florida corporation, has developed and patented low-cost solar collectors that use much less space and produce distilled water at a cost of approximately $3.00 per thousand gallons. They want to try a larger demonstration project that will cost approximately $250,000. They don't have the money. An apparently good idea that should be explored now gathers dust. The Ecological Management Foundation of the Netherlands is working with the

Dutch Applied Research Organization on two techniques for improvement that they believe will reduce the cost of desalination. The chairman of the foundation writes: "Although initial costs for feasibility studies are modest, several million dollars would be required to upscale new technologies to operational proto- types." They're looking for funding, modest indeed compared to the world need. Their foundation believes that desalination "is the best option for avoiding disasters in the next decades."[53] The Lawrence Livermore National Laboratory in California has developed a patented process its scientists believe can reduce energy costs in desalination to a small fraction of their present costs. Experienced scientists there believe it will work. Will it? I don't know, but we should be vigorously pursuing these ideas rather than ignoring them.

Joyce Starr made an excellent suggestion in testimony before a House subcommittee: Establish research awards in this field to attract creative people from around the world to lend their talents to this great need.

.   .   .

While conversion of seawater is still in most cases three to four times as expensive as the traditional freshwater sources, the product of desalination is so pure that it can be blended with the less pure groundwater that may not meet minimum stan- dards either because of salt content or for other reasons. The Virgin Islands are doing that blending now. Often some combi- nation of the converted saltwater and the groundwater will meet minimum standards, saving money for municipalities and water districts that would not know where to turn for relief. Another way to look at desalinated water cost is to compare it with bottled water, which is more than 100 times as expensive per gallon as the desalinated product. (Tests show, incidentally, that people usually can detect no taste difference between the two.) But that comparison with bottled water is deceptive because the price for the desalinated product is still too great to use extensively for agricultural and industrial purposes. That is the goal that must be achieved.

Nationally respected geographer Christopher Lant observes: "If technological breakthroughs greatly reduced the cost of desalinated water. . . . And if desalinated water were to become nearly free, then the world's coastal deserts could become seats of civilization. And since it is energy production technology that would be central to such a breakthrough, and this would apply to water transportation, then inland deserts would join in the bonanza as well. And it would all be environmentally beneficial since it raises the potential of ecosystems and generally counteracts the effects of global warming by fixing carbon in new biomass and, at that enormous scale, potentially lowering sea level. Such dreams are well worth cultivating."[54]

Another more short-term perspective—an encouraging one—is that the cost to the Cypriot government of producing water at their new desalination facility is $1.05 for a cubic meter (about 250 gallons) or $4.20 per 1,000 gallons. That is their *cost*. The domestic freshwater *prices* (higher than cost) for a cubic meter for representative developed nations are the following (1,000 gallon prices in parentheses):

Australia	$1.69	($6.76)
Belgium	$ .85	($3.40)
Canada	$ .43	($1.72)
Finland	$1.02	($4.08)

France	$1.06	($4.24)
Germany	$1.40	($5.60)
Italy	$1.36	($5.44)
United Kingdom	$ .93	($3.72)
United States	$ .53	($2.12)[55]

In many of these nations, some additional add-ons are included either for administrative purposes or for revenue. But the new plant in Cyprus ($4.20 per 1,000 gallons) demonstrates that the cost disparity is narrowing.

Tampa, Florida's, look at water costs (per 1,000 gallons) for the immediate future concluded:

Groundwater	$1.10 to $1.50
Surface water	$1.00 to $1.50
Brackish water	$1.50 to $2.50
Recycled water	$1.50 to $3.90
Desalinated seawater	$3.50 to $4.50[56]

These cost figures are similar to Cyprus's on desalination. The cost of producing freshwater from the sea on Catalina Island in California is approximately $5.00 per 1,000 gallons. By preheating the water, they believe they can cut the costs to $3.80. Though the price will need to come down still more, the successes already achieved are encouraging. Ogden Projects, a large corporation, outlined a plan in Florida to use garbage for energy, applying the landfill costs to reduce water prices, with a result that they claim they can produce desalinated water for $2.50 per 1,000 gallons. At this point that remains theoretical, but ideas like this need to be tried. Ionics Inc. of Watertown, Massachusetts, which built the desalination plant in Santa Barbara,

California, has offered to build and run a Florida plant that will sell water for $3.84 for 1,000 gallons. Those who built the small experimental plant of the Metropolitan Water District in Southern California estimate that they can build a large plant using the demonstration process at a cost of approximately $2.00 for 1,000 gallons. (To give some perspective on what a bargain our citizens have in water, the domestic price of water averages approximately $2.12 for 1,000 gallons. That weighs 8,340 pounds, and the price per ton is 51 cents. What else can you buy that is purified and delivered to your home at 51 cents a ton?)

A lengthy, exhaustive study of the Virginia Beach Quest for Water and the litigation between North Carolina and that city (referred to in Chapter 4) reaches the conclusion that desalination to supplement current supplies of Virginia Beach's sources is sensible and practical.[57]

Malta is dependent on desalinated water for 60 percent of its needs, and the cost is $4.28 per 1,000 gallons. In the Virgin Islands, it costs $7.81 per 1,000 gallons. In oil-rich Saudi Arabia, the price is an artificially low $1.37 to $1.80 per 1,000 gallons. In Bahrain, another oil producer, the cost is $2.14 per 1,000 gallons, and in the Canary Islands, it is $6.14 per 1,000 gallons.

A longer perspective on the cost situation is more encouraging. In the 1950s, desalination cost $15 to $20 per 1,000 gallons; in the 1960s, it dropped to between $5.50 and $9.00 and continued on a decline to as low as $2.00 until energy costs escalated in the 1970s, bringing it up to as high as $7.00. Now costs are generally $4.00 to $6.00, and declining once again. Because of technology improvements, that decline is likely to continue, regardless of energy prices.

Impressive as the cost figures are, even more impressive is another set of statistics: In 1971 the worldwide capacity of desalination plants was 396 *million* gallons a day. By 1996 that reached 5.4 *billion* gallons a day.

Costs are reaching the point where the pioneering Saudi company that is financing the desalination plant in Egypt will be the prototype for many desalination facilities around the world. Private financing is not a substitute for government attention, but it will become a growing method of meeting this need in many nations.

The *National Geographic* put it another way: "To meet the [desalinated water] needs of Israel, Jordan and the West Bank would require less than ten billion dollars [of investment]. By comparison, the gulf war to free Kuwait cost Arab countries $430 billion."[58] The cost of operating a desalinated plant has narrowed, but the capital costs of construction of a desalination plant remain significantly higher—until compared with the cost of possible conflict, and then they are low indeed. The small and limited war in Lebanon (not counting the occupation) cost Israel at least $4 billion. Shimon Peres wrote: "Every day of total war would cost Israel at least $1 billion."[59] That kind of expenditure for desalination facilities and/or research would change the Middle East and the world for the better. Cost per 1,000 gallons also depends on how rapidly capital costs are written off. The Santa Barbara plant, for example, produces desalinated water for $6.00 per 1,000 gallons, but part of that high figure is writing off the capital costs of the plant in only five years.

In an interview, Joyce Starr summed up the situation: "Unlike the computer chip, or the breakthroughs in computer technology, there hasn't been a coalescing of talent [on desalination] and those resources to say, 'Yes, we in the United States can play a major role in helping to save the water future of our planet.' "[60]

It must be done.

8

THE BIG SHORT-TERM PAYOFF:
CONSERVATION

While desalinated water is the great need for our globe over the coming decades and must be pushed *now* to achieve the eventual result of substantially more freshwater for the earth, conserving water through sensible modification of practices can bring results more quickly, as well as help the long run. Sandra Postel puts it this way: "Doing more with less is the first and easiest step along the path toward water security."[1] No one argues with Congressman Rick Boucher of Virginia: "Conservation measures alone will not solve the problem. New sources of freshwater must be developed."[2] But a simple glance at the per capita consumption patterns of nations shows that huge savings can be made by following sensible conservation practices. Iraq uses three times as much water per capita as neighboring Iran; Sudan uses twenty-one times as much as neighboring Ethiopia; Madagascar uses thirty-two times as much as nearby Mozambique; Pakistan uses three times as much as India; Mexico uses six times as much as Guatemala—and the statistics could go on and on.

You don't need to be a water scientist to understand what needs to be done. Several changes are essential.

• In the United States and in countries everywhere, consumers need to be charged the actual cost for bringing them water.

Slight increases in water prices can change our habits fairly easily. Most of us are price sensitive. That is one of the reasons I favor increasing the tax on cigarettes; the higher the tax, the less we will smoke, and the healthier we will be economically and physically.

Until the emergence of a united Germany, West Germany had five times the per capita wealth of East Germany, yet East Germany used four times as much water per capita as its western neighbor because the Communist system contained no price incentives. After the two nations merged and the price structure changed, East German water consumption immediately dropped by one-fourth and is still dropping. One of the reasons Japan's use of water is so low is the high price charged for it. In Bogor, Indonesia, the city increased water fees 30 percent and water demand dropped 29 percent. Sao Paulo, Brazil, initiated effluent charges for industries, and water use by these companies dropped more than 40 percent.

Time magazine reports: "Some farmers in Colorado get their water for . . . one-twentieth the amount it costs neighboring municipalities."[3] And some California farmers pay one-twentieth as much as these Colorado farmers. In the Imperial Valley of California farmers pay an average of $12.50 per acre-foot while a typical home owner in nearby residential areas pays approximately $500 an acre-foot.

When people are charged nothing for water, or farmers get it for as little as one cent per 1,000 gallons, it should surprise no one that water is squandered. It is easy for an author to write, and call for change, but it is difficult for a political leader to achieve if he or she wants to be reelected. However, I believe that if the course of action to be taken is properly explained to people, political courage will be rewarded (if not rewarded in the short run, at least praised in the long run). But what is certain is that political cowardice will have its payback: a damaged earth. When farmers in at least seventeen irrigation districts in the western United States pay less than 1 percent of the cost of bringing water to them, that is unfair to taxpayers and unfair to our water resources. When the cost of water (not the price charged to farmers) is greater than the value of the food produced on the irrigated land, something is askew!

A look at water rates within the United States (as well as in other nations) shows no logic to charges. For example, water-rich Peoria, Illinois, the retail price is more than twice that charged in Phoenix, Arizona. And the uncontested reality from cities and farms, in this country and abroad, is that when prices go up, water consumption goes down. The fastest way to bring about water conservation is to make prices realistic. Secretary of the Interior Bruce Babbitt exaggerated but approached part of the truth when he told the National Press Club in 1993: "If we allow market principles to price water at its true cost, there will be plenty of water for everyone."[4] In a somewhat similar vein, an article in *Forbes* states that transferring 5 percent of agricultural water to urban areas would solve urban needs for the next twenty-five years. That may be technically and theoretically correct, if national boundaries are ignored, but it is extremely difficult to achieve.[5] How could we make progress toward that end? Fair pricing would help. If a grocery store sold some items on sale at below cost, the assumption would be that there must be a surplus of that product. The irony is that water is sold at below cost in much of the world, and we are headed toward a massive shortage.

An interesting effort is being made in Mexico City, which has a high per capita water use, almost double that of most urban areas around the world. Households, accustomed to paying a flat fee, regardless of the amount used, are being metered so that the charge will shift to "more use/more pay." Residents of Mexico City now pay about 30 percent of their water's actual cost. (The World Bank estimate is that developing nations average about 35 percent.) About one-third of the water for Mexico City is pumped eighty-five miles. Mexican officials watched with interest the British experience, where in order to meet European Community treatment standards, the government decided to turn water delivery over to private companies with the understanding that they would charge on the basis of use, and then also treat the water. The British, like Mexico City, generally had fixed charges for residences, regardless of the amount used. The change caused some political protests, when bills suddenly doubled or tripled, but the British government held its ground and soon citizens were installing water-saving devices on showers and toilets and for other domestic uses. Now, to no one's surprise, less water is being used. Whether there will be political will to follow through in Mexico City, where water shortages are much more severe than in Great Britain, is an unanswered question. But so far the process continues in Mexico City and in other areas of that country.

Many cities in our country and many nations charge a flat fee, no matter how much water is used. That includes Reno, Nevada, and parts of Sacramento, California, both in water-hungry states. Why should such consumers be able to water a lawn excessively, or waste irrigation water, or keep the water running while they brush their teeth?

It may be that in some jurisdictions public officials will have to raise the price in a series of steps in order to reach actual costs. If people are paying 25 percent of the costs today, the first step may be to charge 40 percent, a year later 60 percent, and eventually the full cost. It is not as good, in theory, as doing it at once, but it is probably more acceptable politically and would be an easier adjustment for people of limited income. Either way, the net result will be conservation of water resources. Experience suggests that when public officials raise water rates, if that action is combined with some indication of improvement of the water quality, the public accepts the price hike much more readily.

The United States is in far better shape for water than most countries, but approximately one-fourth of the water consumed here is "lost," about three-fourths returned to either groundwater or to surface-water sources. Many nations have a far worse record than we do.[6] As standards of living rise, consumption per capita tends to rise. The U.S. population has more than doubled since the beginning of the century, but our per capita water consumption has increased five to eight times.

One study suggests that an increase in water price of 10 percent in California would decrease agricultural consumption 6.5 percent and overall consumption in the seventeen western states by 3.7 percent, small statistics but huge amounts of water.[7] As water prices for farmers rise, they will shift to crops that produce at least as much income on less water. Fifty percent of the water used by agriculture in California produces only 15 percent of its farm sales. The eastern portion of the United States receives much more rainfall than the west, yet the west consumes 80 percent of the nation's water.

Listen to this comparison of the U.S. and Japan: "The typical American toilet uses three to five gallons of water with each flush, [while] the Japanese toilet . . . flushing mechanism allows the user to choose between two alternative surges of water: a small amount for smaller jobs and a larger amount for larger jobs. In addition, potable water that fills the tank of the Japanese toilet for the next flushing enters through a spigot and a wash basin on the top of the tank. The user can wash his or her hands with clean water that will be reused on the next flushing. The Japanese use this technology because their high water prices provide an incentive to conserve."[8] Combining price increases with efficient plumbing standards for new home construction—standards that decrease the use of water in toilets and showers and in other ways—will result in huge savings in any city, state, or nation. And when less water is used, less water needs to be treated, saving money for the governing entity.

Tucson, Arizona, which has a better water situation than Las Vegas, charges it consumers roughly twice as much for water as Las Vegas does. Scranton, Pennsylvania, charges more than three times as much as Las Vegas. But some of the criticisms of Las Vegas are unwarranted. They charge more for sewer service than most cities, and the waterfalls and water shows at the big casinos generally use recycled, unpurified water, with less than 4 percent of the water of Las Vegas going to this purpose. But even acknowledging that, Las Vegas should be charging more for water. And what is true of Las Vegas is true in many other areas. Rates once designed to encourage agricultural development now encourage water usage that is not sensible. A 1994 national water rate survey by the accounting firm of Ernst and Young shows a crazy-quilt pattern of charges that bears almost no relationship to water scarcity or surplus.

Higher rates have their political problems and sometimes have to be balanced with other considerations. When the Central Arizona Project crossed that state, those who put it together theorized that farmers along the way would help pay for this new water source. But the price established was too high for many farmers, who continued to use the cheaper groundwater. Arizona ended up with the worst of both worlds: depletion of groundwater and diminished income for the Central Arizona Project.

But the overcharging problem of the Central Arizona Project is rare. With few exceptions, governing bodies do not require enough payment from customers to force serious lifestyle modifications that will conserve water. The National Water Survey, a project of the federal government, reports that 91 percent of Nevada's water is consumed by agriculture. All crops in the state are irrigated. Four counties, with only 7 percent of the state's population, have more than 60 percent of the state's irrigated acres. Reduced water usage in these four counties at the other end of Nevada does not automatically translate into more water for Las Vegas. But there is a limited relationship, and having farmers pay adequately for water usage makes sense in Nevada, as it does everywhere.

Another great mistake many water districts make is having a sliding scale for water usage, charging less per 1,000 gallons to those who use more. That practice is common, but it is bad economics and bad environmental policy. For governments at any level to attract an industry by promising low water rates is bad policy that harms an area in the long run. This is a frequent abuse. Geographer Christopher Lant correctly asserts: "Most industrial applications can greatly decrease water use if there is a reason to do so, in effect substituting process changes for water."⁹ The "reason to do so" almost always will be price. Using the mechanism of price, plus government pressure, the former West Germany's industrial consumption of water per capita is approximately one-half the use in the United States. In 1992 Saudi Arabia cut its water rates for small consumers by 50 percent, a politically popular move but not one that serves the long-term interests of that nation. When those who use water are charged realistic rates, the overuse of water diminishes.

The government of Egypt does not want to offend its many farmers, and the government argues, with some validity, that rural life must be kept as attractive as possible so too many people do not move into already-crowded Cairo, so greatly subsidized water rates are used. In Israel, the Water Commission that does the planning and administering of water for the entire country is under the jurisdiction of the Ministry of Agriculture. Because farmers everywhere play such a critical role, all governments like to encourage them, but that encouragement should not be at the cost of wasting water. What the World Bank calls "demand management" is essential.

In some cases the politically prudent method of shifting the burden of raising costs is to sell or lease a water system to a private company. The government receives income in the process and the private company frequently operates with much greater efficiency. When elected officials receive complaints about higher water rates, they can point the finger at the private sector leaders who raised prices, and officials can escape some of the political blame. Buenos Aires has made such a shift, giving a thirty-year contract to a private company that has called for expansion, rehabilitation, and reducing contamination in the old system, with a regulatory body of the city required to approve any rate changes. There is sometimes another advantage to such a move. The World Bank reports: "Inefficient countries typically have ten to twenty employees per 1,000 water connections compared with two to three employees per 1,000 connections in efficient utilities."[10]

Around the world, water rationing is tried only occasionally, and except for severe drought situations, it rarely succeeds. It is not a substitute for imposing realistic prices.

An early Republican draft of a 1995 congressional bill on grazing fees for ranchers on western federal lands is a prime example of what is *not* good policy. Currently, ranchers are charged $1.61 a month for each cow and the same amount for five sheep. The Republican proposal would have had a lifetime exemption from that fee for any "animal that is progeny, born during the period of use authorized under a grazing permit or grazing lease, of an animal on which a grazing fee is paid." In other words, the offspring of those for which farmers currently pay would incur no cost, a bonanza for the ranchers. Catching this not-so-sly piece of special-interest legislation, Representative George Miller of California labeled it "Aid to Families with Dependent Cows." Pointing out that the grazing fee is already far too low, and in two generations the entire system would be free, with tongue-in-cheek he chided his GOP colleagues who are harsh critics of the welfare system for human beings: "It's not good for these cows. They don't have to show any social responsibility. They can just keep having calves. It encourages you to move cows out of the private sector and into the public sector to have their babies just so they can get welfare checks."[11] Embarrassed, the authors of the proposal hastily retreated.

Not only will pricing at actual cost save water, bringing an immediate benefit, but by also raising the cost of freshwater, it helps to make the option of desalinated water more appealing, and that should be a considerable spur to greater investment and research in the major long-term solution.

In the United States, a combination of the increased price of water and an increased emphasis on pollution control (and the cost that goes with that) produced a drop in the industrial water use of 36 percent since 1950, while inflation-adjusted industrial production has increased 3.7 times.[12] However, our per capita water consumption for industrial purposes is far ahead of others, Belgium being in second place, using about one-third less than we do.

Among the people who will benefit most from realistic pricing are not the rich but the poor, who often get poor quality water or no water, paying many times the price of piped water and paying for it also with water diseases. A study by Mark Rosegrant of the International Food Policy Research Institute concluded: "In most countries, water subsidies go disproportionately to the better-off: urban water users connected to the public system and irrigated farmers."[13]

Combining price increases with water-saving ideas is also helpful. The Municipal Water District of Orange County, California, encourages users to "xeriscape" rather than having lawns. The term comes from the Greek word *xeros*, meaning dry. They want users to landscape with plants and rocks that are attractive but use much less water. Half the water used in Orange County homes is for lawns. The water district admonishes its users: "Remember grass means more water. More money. More time. Do not add it unless it will be used for such things as play or entertaining. It certainly will not be put to use [this way] in the front yards." Sunset Books published a 96-page folder, *Waterwise Gardening*, that shows appealing alternatives to lawns (Menlo Park, CA 94025, $7.95). The Metropolitan Water District of Southern

California has published a small free folder, "How to Have a Green Garden in a Dry State" (P.O. Box 54153, Los Angeles, CA 90054). While California homes use more water for lawns than homes in most of the United States, important conservation can occur everywhere, and more of it will occur if water is priced realistically. In an enlightened move, the California legislature in 1983 passed a measure that requires agencies with 3,000 or more water hookups to prepare and adopt plans for more efficient use of water and to update those plans every five years. It is not working miracles, but it helps. Eight states have adopted state plumbing codes designed to save water. In 1989 Connecticut passed three measures calling for greater water conservation and requiring public education on the subject. But the reality is that the fastest, most efficient way to produce conservation of water in significant amounts is to make the price realistic.

Political leaders who give their constituents water at prices below actual costs win temporary applause, but in the long run they hurt their constituents. The reality is that every political leader pays some attention to public opinion, but floating in the wind of public opinion, wherever it leads, is all too common and not leadership.

Listen to this report: "In the early 1990s, water-intensive crops . . . were being grown on 40 percent of California's irrigated cropland, consuming 54 percent of all agricultural water, yet produced only 17 percent of the state's agricultural revenue."[14] An acre of tomatoes uses less water than an acre of rice and brings in ten times as much revenue, although tomatoes require more water than many other fruits and vegetables. California's agricultural expertise meshes with the strong national trend to consume more fresh fruits and fresh vegetables. An increasingly health-conscious America eats roughly 50 percent more of these products per capita than we did twenty-five years ago. And what is good for our health can be good for water conservation.

Rice is the food staple of much of the world, but it is a water-dependent crop. The International Rice Research Institute is working on developing more rice from less water and has already been partially successful by shortening the time that it takes to produce rice. Norman Borlaug, who led the research for the "green revolution" of three decades ago, demonstrated that scientific developments can produce remarkable results and that centuries of traditions in growing crops can be successfully altered. Charging a realistic price for water will hasten rice research and the quick acceptance by farmers of that research.

In October 1997 the World Bank held a briefing on what they called "the El Niño phenomenon." They discussed the global implications of its causes and results. One of those attending made this note: "Current water-related policies are unsustainable financially, environmentally and socially. Only a small percentage of the true cost of water is recovered. We are subsidizing waste of a crucial resource . . . and a big part of the solution will be more reliance on the private sector and assessing the real cost of water. Where that is done, conservation greatly improves."[15]

As the price for water increases even slightly, the disposition of farmers will be to look for production that requires less water. But higher prices alone will not prevent a water catastrophe.

• Pipes that leak badly and irrigation canals and ditches that waste huge amounts of water have to be repaired.

Mexico City loses an estimated one-third of its water through leakage before it reaches the consumers. Egypt could reduce its water usage by at least one-half if it repaired leaky pipes and shifted to drip irrigation. In water-short Jordan, the capital city of Amman has an amazing 59 percent of its water "unaccounted for," meaning that it is losing water through leaks and other structural deficiencies. Syria loses over half its water to ancient irrigation structures and practices, even as the nation experiences frequent cutoffs of water in its two largest cities. In Singapore only 8 percent of the water belongs in the "unaccounted for" category, but in Manila it is 58 percent, and in most Latin American cities it is approximately 40 percent.

The Commonwealth of Puerto Rico serves under an American flag, but its commonwealth status means that it has one nonvoting member in the U.S. House of Representatives and no representation in the Senate, and not surprisingly, its ills are often ignored by the President and Congress because of its lack of political muscle on the Washington scene—despite the fact that it is home to 3.5 million American citizens. Surrounded by ocean water, Puerto Rico declared a water-rationing emergency in 1997 for the second time in three years because of "years of infrastructure neglect coupled with overheated development that has damaged Puerto Rico's drinking reservoirs and polluted their water," the *Washington Post* reported.[16] The article says that the island is losing up to 45 percent of its treated drinking water.

To assure that water gets where it is needed and that it is utilized effectively, small irrigation canals can be lined with plastic. Larger irrigation canals can be made of concrete for the same reasons. Making sensible changes to harness the tools of irrigation is vital. Irrigation for most farmers has not changed in 2,000 years. It must change. While only 15 percent of the world's cropland is irrigated, the irrigated portions produce up to half of the world's food.

As the water travels in irrigation canals or ditches, much of it is absorbed by the earth. If it is water that fell in the form of rain, it is virtually salt-free. But as it moves over the ground, the water absorbs salt, as well as pollutants that farmers use to encourage production. When the water gets to the cropland, it leaves the saline residue it absorbed in transit. Pakistan, which irrigates three-fourths of its arable land, now has large areas that no longer provide agricultural production because of the saline residue from irrigation. And from Africa to Pakistan there are "salt lakes," remains of what had been lakes where salt accumulated and the water gradually disappeared. Countries like Israel and Tunisia, which have followed careful irrigation policies and used channels protected from salt and pollutants in ground soil, have substantially increased food production on less water. But nations like Pakistan, where irrigation practices have not been good, are producing less per acre, primarily because of problems due to salt. Tanzania, Mozambique, Sudan, and Nigeria also fall into this category.

In addition to structural protection of water, more careful use when it gets to its destination is required. The irrigation system in a development called Westpark in California is electronically tied to the University of California weather station. When the land needs water, it receives and uses it, but not otherwise. With only 15 percent of the development covered, the savings in water, ironically, is 15 percent.

Israel developed drip irrigation: plastic pipes or small tubes, either buried or aboveground, with holes that are monitored by computers so that the amount of water provided for crops is not wasted. Farmers watering fields through traditional irrigation, using their instinct and experience, worked in a water-surplus world and water-surplus areas. But Israeli farmers who irrigate have doubled their production in twenty years using the same amount of water. Well over half of Israel's cropland now uses drip irrigation. And farmers from Jordan to California are following this good example. Its use will continue to spread. Listen to this report from two predominantly Muslim nations that are using the drip irrigation developed by Israel: "Projects in Kazakhstan and Uzbekistan reportedly have increased crop yields several-fold while cutting water consumption by two-thirds."[17] The difficulty with drip irrigation is that it is expensive and needs an assured supply of water. Not having drip irrigation can be even more expensive, however, sometimes not to the individual farmer. The world should be grateful to Israel for this research. A somewhat similar development by Israel, micro-sprinklers—also run by computers—dramatically reduce the loss of water through evaporation from either the standard sprinklers or the ancient but still prevailing method of open-ditch irrigation. They also reduce the saline residue. The Research Institute at King Fahd University in Saudi Arabia is experimenting with everything from methods to more effectively use water to finding crops that require less of it to desalination. Syria has a research center that focuses on developing crops that require less water.

Water savings through techniques from drip irrigation to computer irrigation tied into weather predictions are not totally unmixed blessings. When water is not "wasted," then less of it ultimately flows back into rivers and streams and aquifers. But, on balance, these developments in irrigation are largely beneficial to humanity and conserve what, next to air, is our most essential resource.

• Reusing water is both safe and needed, even though some find it aesthetically unpleasing.

Only a small percentage of our water is recycled, but the practice is growing. The pioneer in the United States is Phoenix, Arizona, which reclaims 80 percent of its wastewater. In Israel and Saudi Arabia 40 percent of their water is recycled, and they are dissatisfied with that percentage. Approximately 10 percent of U.S. manufacturers now recycle—a term some prefer to reuse—not a high figure, but five times higher than forty years ago. Japan is far ahead of other nations. It has a Water Re-Use Promotion Center. Japanese industries recycle 76 percent of their water, some industries achieving rates as high as 92 percent.

Listen to this State of Nevada report: "Currently effluent from 21 wastewater treatment plants [out of 181] throughout the State is reclaimed and reused for applications such as golf course and landscape irrigation, crop and pasture irrigation, power plant cooling water, sand and gravel processing, and construction water."[18] Nevada does not have the luxury of choosing whether it will do better; it must. Nevada is one of eight states that have adopted state plumbing codes with the aim of conservation and water reuse.

Conservation practices, recycling, and education can help, illustrated by Clark County Nevada's per capita usage: In 1989 they used 352 gallons per capita each day; in 1990 they used 337 gallons, a drop of 15 gallons per person, multiplied by 365 days a year. This is no small reduction—and they can do better. They will have to. Charging more for water will create greater savings.

California and Florida are ahead of other states in water reuse, but this practice is still in its infancy in the United States and in most nations. Water recycling has been a measurable but small factor in the United States for about thirty years. Reusing water from sewers, for example, is not at first blush aesthetically pleasing, but if properly treated is safe. The aesthetic difficulty is that people simply react negatively to the thought that they are drinking or bathing in water that has been used for sewage disposal. There are no technical barriers to properly treating such water and reusing it, though it can be costly. In Orange County, California, aquifers are being recharged with treated, reclaimed water both to sustain the aquifers and to prevent the ever-present danger of seawater intrusion. The wells into which the water is injected are 3.5 miles from the Pacific Ocean.

St. Petersburg, Florida, has a dual water distribution system that uses recovered water for commercial developments and other limited purposes. It says it has the largest reclaimed water system in the world, distributing approximately 26 million gallons a day of water for reuse. Cape Coral, Florida, utilizes reused water for lawns and fire protection.

The significance of water reuse for industrial and agricultural purposes is especially important because it takes 7,060 gallons of water to produce a ton of milk, 30,000 gallons of water for a ton of meat, 138,000 gallons for a ton of beet sugar, 291,000 gallons for a ton of textiles, 410,000 gallons for a ton of aluminum, 462,000 gallons for a ton of synthetic rubber, and 543,000 pounds for a ton of paper. Recycled paper takes "only" 27,500 gallons, and as an added bonus, saves trees. If we want to maintain or improve our standard of living, water recycling will have to play a much bigger part in our future.

The *California Water 2020* report calls for at least five times as much water reuse in that state in the next two decades. Reuse will be part of the future for California and the rest of the world.

• Aquifers must be monitored and guarded carefully.

Middle East water expert Joyce Starr refers to what is happening to the aquifers there as "Armageddon underground."[19] A 1994 report of the U.S. Agency for International Development notes: "Gaza exceeds its renewable supplies by 50 percent every year, resulting in serious saltwater intrusion [of its groundwater]."[20] Shallow aquifers can be replenished by rain, but deep ones cannot. The Gaza aquifer is near complete depletion. Israel has discovered new aquifers by drilling more deeply, although there is divided opinion on the size of these finds and the quality of the water. One study of several countries concludes: "Saudi Arabia, Kuwait, Qatar and Bahrain are using nonrenewable groundwater resources in large quantities, causing depletion of this valuable resource and deterioration in water quality."[21]

The same could be written about almost every Middle East nation. In the United Arab Emirates, the water table has dropped eighteen to sixty feet in eight years. The Global Water Policy Project estimates that Saudi Arabia is using groundwater at almost three times its renewal rate. Egypt and Saudi Arabia hope to discover new aquifers, but in the meantime, the gradual harm being done by excessive use, by seawater seepage, compounded by population growth, spells trouble for the future. Untreated sewage is entering some aquifers. Lowering aquifers almost always means declining quality of the water extracted, and with the exception of desalinated water, Middle Eastern water is already below the standards of Europe.

A British expert in this area writes: "In order to green the desert, these [Middle East] states are tapping aquifers and exploiting them far faster than they can be replenished."[22] Add to this an unsettled political climate where nations that share aquifers may find difficulty agreeing on anything, much less the essential and volatile issue of water, and the importance of prudence is clear. When an aquifer crosses national boundaries, and that is often the case, tensions rise when one country perceives that its water is being used by another nation.

But it is not just in the Middle East where aquifers are being depleted. The situation there is more dramatic and will more quickly reach a climax but all over the United States and in most other nations aquifers are being depleted. A front-page story in the *Washington Post* has a heading that tells the story: "Local Aquifers Are Being Pressed to Their Limits as Development Floods Rural Areas."[23]

Here is a description of the Snake River aquifer in Idaho: "The large rate and quantity of withdrawals has affected the flows of springs, rivers, and streams. Every gallon pumped from the aquifer in some way impacts water available to surface water sources. Unfortunately, the state has never known how much water is withdrawn or diverted, how much is consumptively used and how much returns to the rivers or percolates back to the aquifer."[24] The Snake River aquifer is somewhat typical. It is being depleted, and harm is being done. However, aquifers are not easily measured; although we know damage is taking place, no one really knows how much.

The importance of monitoring and conserving underground water is underscored by the fact that 39 percent of this nation's public water supply is from groundwater.

Stanford's Paul and Anne Ehrlich describe part of this problem:

In California's San Joaquin Valley, aquifers are being pumped at a rate that exceeds recharge by more than 500 billion gallons annually—and the rate is rising. That enormous overdraft to

143

support irrigation in one California valley is difficult to visualize. It can perhaps best be pictured as roughly double the flow of oil into the American economy each year.

Listen to the words of Mike Personett, a water specialist:

Much of the water of the Ogallala [aquifer] can be considered "fossil" water in that it was laid down many thousands of years ago during an ice age. Natural recharge to the formation is very low. . . . The Ogallala can be likened to a seam of coal. Any significant use of the water in the Ogallala will result in mining. Managing the Ogallala on a safe yield basis would essentially eliminate all but municipal and industrial use.[25]

He has good news also: Price increases in Texas for using the aquifer reduced agricultural consumption by more than 28 percent. But the overall picture of the Ogallala and of aquifers all over the globe, with few exceptions, is one of gradual, and frequently rapid, depletion. The Ogallala, the biggest aquifer in our country, is not about to be drained in the next decade or two decades, but the trend is clear. As a story in the *National Geographic* notes: "If the aquifer were completely drained, it would take up to 6,000 years to refill."[26] Nebraska has access to far more of the Ogallala's water than any state, but the Ogallala's waters are significant in seven other states. In the last half century the water table of the Ogallala has declined as little as ten feet in some areas, but as much as 100 feet in others. Kansas has pumped 40 percent of its share of the Ogallala water. Kansas will change dramatically if that trend line does not stabilize or reverse itself. Even today, a lower water table means that farmers have to spend more money pumping out the water, and as aquifer levels decline, so gradually does the quality of the product.

Here is Marc Reisner's report on two areas: "In 1914, there were 139 irrigation wells in all of West Texas. In 1937, there were 1,166. In 1954, there were 27,983. In 1971, there were 66,144. Nebraska irrigated fewer than a million acres in 1959. In 1977, it irrigated nearly seven million acres; the difference was almost entirely pumped from the Ogallala."[27]

• **Conservation plans must include development of energy resources that save water and do not warm the earth more through the greenhouse effect.**

The obvious area for greater experimentation is solar energy, already discussed. Breakthroughs in solar energy would decrease water and air pollution dramatically.

Safer nuclear energy is another possibility. I voted against the Price-Anderson measure that limits the liability of the nuclear energy industry, a protection no other industry has. Backers said they needed it to develop the program. My guess is that if we had proceeded with a little more caution, we might have developed better nuclear answers earlier. The present nuclear energy process has the still-unsolved problems of what to do with the spent fuel and the environmental hazard it represents, as well as the danger that this radioactive by-product may be used for nuclear weapons production. In response to this, the environmental community understandably has responded negatively to further nuclear development. That logical response, however, carried over into opposition to research into the development of much safer nuclear energy. The antinuclear sentiment within the environmental community did not distinguish between what is logical and what is not logical. The Argonne Laboratories were apparently successfully developing a nuclear energy form that had neither of the two major drawbacks of residue and weapons threats. The environmental movement should have been supporting it, but it did not, and the White House caved in to demands to halt the research. It is at least temporarily dead. Starting it again would be expensive, both in time—because scientists who had been developing this have since scattered to a variety of other opportunities—and money. But somewhere, somehow, sensible research should commence again.

We know the power of the ocean tides, and precisely when they roll in and out. That has great potential for creating energy, and it is now taking place on an experimental basis in the Bay of Fundy in Canada and at the mouth of the La Rance River in France. It does not have the potential to develop into an energy factor as important as solar power, but the potential is there for contributing a substantial amount of energy in an environmentally safe manner.

Discussed also in Chapter 7, traditional utilities often have on-site waste of power. Also, anyone who drives past an oil refinery will see the waste heat being burned, doing nothing for anyone. In some cases these waste products can be harnessed to assist the desalination process, and in more and more instances, that is now happening.

.   .   .

The bottom line on all of this is that the fast way to halt the hemorrhaging of our water supply is to apply the first aid of conservation. The patient, our world, can then limit its self-inflicted damage while we work feverishly to further develop the transfusion that will be needed, desalinated water.

9

POLLUTION COMPLICATES
EVERYTHING

No one can look at the world's water supply without noting the connection between water quality and water quantity. Water quality and water quantity problems cannot be separated. Water that is too polluted cannot be used for households, agriculture, or industry. Pollution is, in effect, another form of consumption—only more destructive than the others. Technically, of course, it is not consumption, but when toxic substances make water unfit for human, agricultural or industrial use, the result is the same as consumption—only worse. Polluted water that cannot be used continues to flow, into lakes and rivers, into the ocean, degrading the water that ultimately will have to be used.

Polluted water kills and destroys by denying this resource to people who need it, and it kills by carrying disease and devastation. Death by diarrhea, common in most of the world, is caused by polluted water. So are most of the other major killers in the poorer nations. A *New York Times* front-page headline tells the story: "For Third World, Water Is Still a Deadly Drink."[1] Unfortunately it is also essential for survival. Eighty percent of the diseases in developing nations are water-borne. If those who read these words (and this author) do not energize ourselves a little to ensure that others in the world have clean water, then we share in the guilt for this preventable tragedy. We are the managers, caretakers if you will, of this earth and we have the responsibility to pass it on to future generations in an undevastated form.

While all harmful pollutants need to be restricted or eliminated, the pollutant that does the most harm is one with which we are familiar and all use: salt.

Aquifers that have provided relatively safe water and then are overused become too salty for human consumption. Thirsty people must then rely on less safe sources that cause disease and death. Groundwater sources that are too near the ocean experience salt penetration as the freshwater is removed. Salt devastates cropland, when water that is too salty is used for irrigation. It is difficult to believe that a product that looks so benign on our dining room tables can cause such devastation. But it does.

Much of the world's water supply is unsafe—more than three-fifths of the world's homes hand-carry water from outside sources—and most of the world's population does not have basic health protection that even primitive sewer facilities bring, health protection that is within our means and our knowledge.

Positive things can happen.

In an impoverished area of Karachi, Pakistan, known as Orangi, Dr. Akhter Hameed Khan, a respected community organizer, talked to people about what they wanted, and the answer came back clearly: sewer service. He and community members organized, explained to people what sanitation services could do to improve their lives, got commitments from people to help in the manual labor necessary, and the total cost for a sanitary house latrine, plus underground sewers, amounted to less than $100 per household. Now 600,000 poor people in Karachi have primitive sewer service, and they and their more prosperous neighbors have a better chance for good health.

In Sao Paulo, Brazil, the poor settlement/squatter areas know as *favelas* had piped water to only 32 percent of the residents, and less than 1 percent had sewer system connections. The fall of the military dictatorship in 1985 gave these people a voice and they appealed to authorities for water and sewers. A decade later 99 percent of these people have piped water and 15 percent have sewer hookups—still some distance to go, but a huge improvement in the lives of most of them. Again, as in Karachi, it would not have happened without dedicated and creative leadership.

In the last two years in Ethiopia, 155,000 more people now have piped water, an increase from 20 percent of the population to 21 percent.

The positive stories are good—but few. Most urban centers in the developing world either have no sewer system, or one that serves only the wealthiest of its citizens. Most human excrement and other forms of waste are untreated and end up in open ditches, rivers, streams, and lakes, or even worse, collecting in small pools of stagnant water, where insects that carry life-threatening and debilitating diseases breed. The metropolitan area of Monterrey, Mexico, for example, has almost 3 million people but none of the wastewater it collects is treated. Nationally, less than 12 percent of Mexico's urban wastewater is treated before discharge. Five states in Mexico have *no* wastewater treatment.

Lake Victoria in Africa is that continent's largest freshwater body of water. But the quality is deteriorating as Kenya, Tanzania, and Uganda dump raw sewage into it.

Guinea worm disease is not life-threatening, but the water-carried disease causes its victims six weeks of illness. Thanks to the leadership of former President Jimmy Carter and the center that bears his name in Atlanta, and the cooperation of the DuPont Corporation, guinea worm disease is being dramatically reduced. Focusing on one disease and stopping it is a great contribution, but it is not a substitute for focusing on cleaner water and adequate sanitation facilities so that this disease and a host of others can be eliminated. Between 1980 and 1990, the number of Africans without safe drinking water increased by *at least* forty million, and the number not covered by sanitation service increased by at least 120 million, probably much more. Forty-two percent of the people of Nicaragua in Central America do not have safe drinking water. And that is better than most developing nations, which average 56 percent without safe drinking water. To have 2 million children under the age of five die of diarrhea each year—almost always caused by bad water—ought to trouble the consciences of all of us who are more fortunate, but we hardly notice.

The lead story in a 1996 *Chicago Tribune* article is headed: "Arsenic in Water Poisoning Millions."[2] This is not a story of millions of people swallowing arsenic pills and suddenly dying. That would have made global news. This is a story by an enterprising reporter, Paul Salopek, who found people in India and Bangladesh with "purplish scabs . . . palms cracking and bleeding . . . headaches, chest congestions and stomach cramps." And, of course, in many cases, death resulted, caused by arsenic residue from closed mining operations that found its way into the groundwater. The United States has experienced a little of this in some of our western mining towns. Pour toxic substances into the ground anywhere—do it in the middle of a desert—and eventually water will pick them up. The *Tribune* story includes a picture of a ten-year-old girl who her doctor says will live less than a year. She is shown pumping water from the well that is killing her.

Almost everywhere farmers now understand that if you pour untreated human waste onto a field of vegetables or other crops, the resulting food production can cause great harm. But when water sources run dry and farmers see no alternative, they utilize what they know to be a long-term danger simply to survive. That complicates all the other problems. Even "safe" water that most of the world's farmers use is not very safe. That does not mean that sewage that contains human waste cannot be treated and used without harm. It can. And for some purposes, fish farming as an example, apparently both untreated human and animal waste can be used to feed fish in sequestered ponds, which can then safely be used for human consumption.

However, generally untreated sewage represents a serious threat. Everywhere. When you drive through a residential area of Alexandria in Egypt, a car sends up spray—not from water blown in from the ocean, not from leaking water pipes, not from rainfall, but from sewage that goes into the street from apartment buildings.

On the revered Ganges River in India 114 cities, each with more than a population of 50,000, dump untreated sewage into the river each day. Listen to this story about a mother in India:

Usha Bhagwani, a rail-thin 28-year-old housemaid points out [her] children and frets about how to spend their [family's] rupees. Should they buy good food so that the children will get stronger? Or should they buy shoes so that the children will not get hookworms? Or should they buy kerosene to boil the water?

There is not enough money for all of those needs, so parents must choose. It was to save money, as well as to save time, that Mrs. Bhagwani was serving unboiled water to her 5- and 7-year old boys in her one-room hovel. . . .

The water has already killed two of her children, a 15-month-old, Santosh, a boy who died two years ago, and Sheetal, a frail 7-month-old girl who died just a few months ago. But everyone in the slum drinks the water, usually without boiling, and water seems so natural and nurturing that Mrs. Bhagwani does not understand the menace it contains.

"I try to boil the water," Mrs. Bhagwani said pleasantly. "But the boys sometimes insist on drinking right away because they're thirsty."

Then, she said, there is the cost. To boil water consistently would cost about $4 a month in kerosene, almost a third of Mrs. Bhagwani's earnings. She could afford that, but then there would be less money for food.[3]

The same article tells of a woman in a village in Cambodia. She gets water from a pond. The story relates what is true for this woman and for much of the world: "The villagers bathe in the pond, and cattle use it as well. Moreover, since there is no toilet, the water is probably contaminated with human waste." Situations like these are responsible for the recent resurgence of malaria. Stagnant water breeds the mosquitoes that carry it. The world now spends a grand total of approximately two cents per case to deal with malaria. The World Health Organization estimates that 2.7 million people a year contract it.

A British charitable organization, WaterAid (1 Queen Anne's Gate, London SW1H 9BT), placed full-page advertisements in several publications there. Its heading reads: "Safe Water Is the

Foundation for Health and Health Is the Foundation for Development." The body of the ad includes:

> Water is essential. No one can survive without it. For millions of the world's poorest people, fetching water for their daily needs means a long walk, often to a polluted source. Poor sanitation makes a bad situation worse. . . . Ten million children will die unnecessarily this year from illnesses which can be averted by basic improvements to water supplies and sanitation. WaterAid is a charity which helps communities to build their own safe water supplies. . . . 10 [British pounds] buys a spade to dig wells; 45 [British pounds] a ton of cement to line them. Your support will make a lasting contribution. Already 1.5 million [people] have benefitted.

Even a relatively modern nation like Lebanon has a water and sewage system that one writer describes as "overloaded, poorly maintained, and far from meeting basic sanitation requirements."[4]

What makes all of these situations tragic is their needlessness. By 500 B.C. the Romans had built extensive aqueducts, still in existence today, and had an enclosed sewage system that functioned effectively. It should not take us 2,500 years to bring what existed in Rome to all of the urban centers of the world. The British parliament established the first sewage district in the world in 1856, moved by the stench of the River Thames. What Rome had 2,500 years ago, what London had 140 years ago, we must now bring to all population centers if we are serious about stemming disease and bringing quality life to all humanity. And today, more than at any other time in human history, diseases cross national boundaries because of travel and international trade.

The list of bodies of water that are badly polluted is almost endless, as are other basic sanitary needs. Just as one small example: Hundreds—probably thousands—of hospitals in developing nations have "outhouses" for their toilet facilities.

The United States is, of course, not immune to pollution problems. The 1990 census shows that in federally designated "Persistent Poverty Counties," 4.6 percent of the households do not have indoor toilets. At least forty-three places on the Great Lakes are not considered safe for swimming or fishing. Not too many years ago, our citizens were stunned to learn about the Cuyahoga River, so badly polluted that it caught on fire. Fortunately, that situation has improved. In 1997 a toxic microbe called *Pfiesteria piscicida* invaded Chesapeake Bay, causing fish infection. Officials closed three tributaries in Maryland and one river in Virginia to all fishing, swimming, and boating. Two large lakes created in the western United States, Lake Powell and Lake Mead, have serious problems due to boaters and campers simply dumping their waste. The Associated Press reports: "The uninhibited dumping has resulted in dangerous levels of fecal coliform bacteria at both lakes. Coliform bacteria, which multiply in human waste, can cause diarrhea, nausea, headaches, fatigue, and jaundice."[5]

Public perception suggests that pollution is caused by industries, and that is partially correct. But we are all part of it. Our cars. Our homes. Our lawnmowers. Our boats. Our farms. When airplanes or strong blowers apply pesticides to cropland, there is a tendency for those pesticides to travel beyond the intended farmland and eventually into nearby streams. It is estimated that half the water wells in the nation have nitrates. These nitrates generally come from agricultural fertilizers, and when there are too many nitrates the oxygen supply in lakes and streams and wells suffers. Most of the pollution in the United States is what is called "non-point pollution," meaning the source of it cannot be precisely pin-pointed. Most non-point pollution comes from agriculturally related sources. Harm to lakes and streams and wells from agricultural pesticides and industrial waste tends to be more of a problem in developed nations like the United States than in the developing world.

Many cities in our nation do not have separate storm sewers to handle sudden rainfalls. A heavy rain causes either backup of sewage in homes and businesses, or more likely, the sewage treatment plant is built to handle a certain level and when that level is exceeded, raw sewage goes into the stream. Even places that have storm sewers often are unprepared. Chicago is improving its dual system, but a heavy rain today results in raw sewage being dumped into Lake Michigan or the Illinois River. Narragansett Bay in Rhode Island cannot handle more than one inch of rain. More than that causes direct sewage dumping into the bay. Approximately 2.5 billion gallons of raw sewage flow into the bay each year, closing about one-fourth of the bay to shellfishing.[6] Not surprisingly, water-borne diseases in our country have increased, not decreased, since 1971. Even without the overload problem, separate storm drainage that ordinarily does not call for treatment, means that oil and other residues on the streets are poured untreated into streams.

While the United States needs to do more, we have made progress on everything from no-lead gasoline use (and more miles per gallon) to significant increases in expenditures for pollution control. If we were an island unto ourselves, unaffected by what happens in the rest of the world, we could take satisfaction in what we have done, even though some nations have done better. Sweden inaugurated tight conservation and pollution controls. The net result: water use cut in half while industrial production doubled during the same time period.

In our country, every state has problems. Rhode Island would seem to be the least likely to have difficulties with water quality. It is a wealthy, compact state. Yet a 1995 survey by the U.S. Department of Agriculture found sixteen communities with water quality problems. All are small communities, but the 2,200 households in the community of Orange in Franklin County should be entitled to pure water as much as the people of urban Providence.

A 1995 study by the Natural Resources Defense Council attributes 1,200 deaths a year in the United States to poor quality water.

Beach closings because of pollution problems in our country increased 50 percent in 1996 over 1995. The increase to 3,522 closings and warnings in 1996 occurred principally in California and Florida, states with long coastlines. The major cause: heavy rains that caused untreated sewage to go into the ocean.

Places with shallow aquifers should be careful about pollution. The Florida 1995 Water Plan states: "Groundwater in Florida is particularly vulnerable to contamination. The state is covered nearly everywhere by a thin layer of surficial sands that overlie a thick sequence of porous limestone and dolomite. Depth of groundwater throughout the state is relatively shallow."[7] In laymen's language, that means Floridians have to be more careful in avoiding pollution than the residents of any other state, with the possible exception of Hawaii.

An example of what can be done about lack of proper sewage treatment can be seen in Lesotho, in the southern part of Africa. A country with 1.8 million people, and a life expectancy of fifty-six years, local officials working with United Nations agencies are promoting ventilated pit latrines in schools and in residential areas, combined with a sewage system in some instances. Residents apply for a loan to be repaid over a period of twenty months or longer. To be eligible, the applicant has to be eighteen years of age and has to "collect 120 blocks and sand for the substructure. You must also dig your own pit."[8] Trained builders are available for advice. The World Bank reports that the program is working. It will probably extend the average life span, diminish pollution of nearby lakes and streams, dramatically reduce pools of badly polluted stagnant water, and make the water that is available more usable for irrigation and other purposes.

One of the great myths, fostered by those who oppose making changes to protect our earth, is that such steps are economically harmful. They could be, if carried to extremes, but that is almost never the case. Listen to Gregg Easterbrook: "Environmental regulations, far from being burdensome and expensive, have proved to be strikingly effective, have cost less than was anticipated, and have made the economies of the countries that have put them into effect stronger, not weaker."[9] Secretary of State Warren Christopher told a Stanford University audience: "Protecting the environment opens new business opportunities. We are committed to helping U.S. companies expand their already commanding share of a $400 billion market for environmental technologies."[10]

The oceans must be protected.

More than thirty years ago, I saw something I can remember vividly to this day: a truck in El Salvador loaded with garbage, backing up and dumping its load over a cliff into the ocean. That truck symbolizes what we are doing to the ocean every day, even though we usually do it silently and less dramatically.

Fouling the ocean with our human and agricultural and industrial waste harms our future source of water and our current and future source of food. Some even advocate dumping nuclear wastes into the ocean, which has to be about as short-sighted a policy as can be imagined.

Scientists accurately equate our globe with the human body. They say that the earth has two lungs: the oceans and the forests. When we pollute the former and reduce the latter, we foul the clean breathing apparatus of the planet on which we live.

We now get food in the ocean the way we once found food on land—by hunting for it. We call it fishing. And like the land hunt for bison and other species, we are reducing and eliminating some species of fish because of overfishing. The world takes four and one half times as much tonnage of fish from the ocean each year as we did forty years ago. An article in *Newsweek* observes: "The oceans that once seemed a bottomless source of high-protein, low-fat food are rapidly being depleted."[11]

Not only are we harming our current supply of food, the time will come when we must "farm" the ocean just as we grow crops on land. The growing world population eventually will dictate it. One acre of ocean, for example, can grow 340,000 pounds of high-protein mussels. But aquatic life—particularly shellfish—absorbs the poisons we dump into the ocean. We cannot pollute the sea and expect to safely feed ourselves from it. Most fish live in areas near the land mass, and that is the same area into which our often-polluted rivers flow. As the world population grows, the discharge of raw sewage into rivers, and ultimately into the ocean, is an increasing problem. Ships and boats also are major polluters, as anyone who has walked along an ocean beach discovers.

The nature of ocean contaminants has changed as our culture has. Discharges from hospitals, everything from needles to unused or unusable medicines, find their way into the ocean. The winds that once carried dust from dry cropland and sand from the deserts now also carry industrial wastes into the ocean, sometimes thousands of miles from their point of origin. One study notes: "Every year, about 1,000 new chemicals join the ranks of 65,000 chemicals already available to industry and agriculture. About 10,000 of these chemicals are regularly used in some agricultural or industrial process. Little is known about what happens to such chemicals when they enter water."[12] One estimate is that 40 percent of ocean pollution is from river runoff, 30 percent from the wind, 10 percent from direct land-based dumping into the ocean and the balance from ships and other sources.[13] And again, a growing population compounds all these difficulties.

Part of protecting the oceans is to know as much about them as possible. Sylvia Earle, author and former chief scientist at the National Oceanographic and Atmospheric Administration, claims that we know more about Mars than we know about the oceans.[14] That is an exaggeration, but it points to the deficiency of our research on the oceans, particularly at great depths.

Part of research on the seas should include scientific inquiry on how to handle unusual pollution problems, such as an oil spill, or a mercury dumping, like the one that occurred in Minamata Bay in Japan. The best answer is to *prevent* the damage to the ocean and the community of nations can do a much better job of that. The oceans, because of their immense size, are generally more pollution-free per cubic meter than the surface waters we use for consumption. But we need more knowledge on how to deal with catastrophes as we gradually become increasingly dependent on our oceans.

10

DEALING WITH
POPULATION AND . . .

There are other important ways to deal with the water crisis that are by no means incidental. As is the case with most major issues, the solutions to the problem are complex, and the answer is a mosaic, with no single, easy, dramatic remedy. We will have to work on all fronts simultaneously: desalination research and development, conservation, pollution control, and at least four more basic issues.

• Population control.
_____

More people consume more water. And as their average standard of living rises, which is generally the case up to this point, water consumption increases more rapidly than the population growth would indicate. Whatever can humanely retard population growth will help protect our usable water supply.

The highly respected Population Institute predicts a doubling of the world population in forty years. Most forecasts suggest doubling will take place in approximately fifty or more years, a few stretching it to sixty years and beyond. Even the few people who say that population growth is no problem—and they are few indeed—recognize that the earth's people will soon increase by at least a factor of two. There are already 1.5 billion people who live in abject poverty, a condition far worse than the U.S. standard for poverty. The World Bank reports that 1.3 billion people live on less than one dollar a day. As the world's population grows, it is highly probable—but not certain—that those statistics will get worse.

There is some good news on the population front. Approximately 44 percent of the world's population now lives in countries that have a fertility rate at or below the replacement level. Over the last two decades the average number of births for a woman has declined from 4.5 to 3.1. Zero population growth is slightly over 2.0. But balancing these good numbers are increases in life expectancy.

If there can be a further slowing of birth rates around the world, that will help reduce the population numbers eventually and partially compensate for our life expectancy being extended. A century ago the life expectancy of the average American was forty-eight years. Today it is seventy-six. Two scholars in this field, James Vaupel of the University of Minnesota and John Owen of Duke, believe that for a child born in 1984 or later, the life expectancy is now ninety to one hundred years. To estimate the world's population, life expectancy has to be combined with the birth rate. The difference in water demand between a world with 11 billion people or 12 billion people is staggering. Unfortunately, we will be dealing with those kind of figures within the lifetime of a twenty-year-old who reads these words.

For almost all of human history, the earth's population was never more than 10 million. By 1830 it reached 1 billion, and a century later that figure had doubled. I was born about that time, in 1928. I have seen the world population almost triple, and if the actuarial tables are accurate in my case, I will see it quadruple in one lifetime.

Jonathon Cole of the Institute of Ecosystem Studies says that a doubling of the world population—and he accepts the forty-year estimate—will produce at least a 55 percent increase in nitrates entering our water, nitrates that feed algae that suck oxygen from the water, damaging animal life in the oceans and rivers and lakes, among other harmful results.[1] A combination of overfishing and nitrates could have a devastating impact on nations heavily dependent on fish for consumption. In the Philippines, for example, the average per capita fish consumption is ninety pounds per year. Already, their fish catch is down from earlier years, and they are expected to double their population in the next quarter century. Where will they get the food?

The United States has been guilty of one of the most short-sighted actions possible: cutting back money for family planning. While we have made clear that no federal funding can go for abortions, an understandable limitation, why we cut back on something as vital as family planning is beyond my comprehension. Opponents do not seem to understand this reality: More unwanted children result in more abortions, in any country. It is inspiring to visit a nation like Tunisia, as one example, and see what a great job that government is doing to get the word out to women and men about the importance of family planning, and how they can achieve it. We should be aiding these efforts which are in the interest of developing nations and in our interest as well. Less than 3 percent of our foreign aid goes for family planning. When I hear speeches on the floor of the House and Senate condemning the United Nations Population Fund and its "bloated bureaucracy," I know that some ill-informed fiction writer must be on the staff of that member. That "bloated bureaucracy" has a total of 166 employees to help reduce the flood of humanity that is engulfing the entire world. If there is criticism, it should be that their staff and efforts are much too small in comparison with the importance and the enormity of the task that is so critical to all of civilization. No one seriously questions the reality that when people are provided with family planning information, the birth rate drops, often dramatically.[2] Statistics from country after country verify this. The population director for CARE reports that family planning programs "have slowed population growth in developing nations by one-third since 1971. Without these programs, an additional 400 million people would now inhabit the earth. . . . Contraceptive use by married women in the developing world was 10 percent in 1965. Today it is above 50 percent."[3] That good news is accompanied by the other good news that we are extending life, but that also means huge population growth. For example, while India's birth rate is down, its citizens are living longer, and that one nation alone adds 16 million people a year to its population. If we cannot provide safe water and sewers for most of the world's population now, where will we be forty or fifty years from now, when twice as many people inhabit our globe? Encouraging voluntary family planning is humanitarian, it is prudent, and it helps to protect all of the world's population.

While almost all the growth in population in the coming decades will be in the developing nations, population expansion in the more prosperous nations is also serious, because on a per capita basis we consume so much more water and energy and all of the other natural resources, and we pollute much more. A child born in the United States today is expected to produce fifty-two tons of garbage by the age of seventy-five, use five times the energy of a child born in the developing world, and consume 10 million gallons of water.[4]

Almost all new homes built in the United States include a dishwasher and a washing machine for laundry, things most people in the developing nations have never seen. (It is encouraging to read an advertisement for a washer that reads: "In comparison to an average conventional washer, nine loads per week, a Maytag Neptune saves 6,752 gallons per year." Maytag boasts that their washer requires "nearly half the water of many conventional washers.") Most kitchen and laundry conveniences use a great deal of water.

The lack of equity in the distribution of wealth in the world is not the subject of this book, but it is in itself potentially explosive, and the inequitable distribution of the shrinking amount of usable water—to use a bad metaphor—simply adds fuel to that fire. The global share of income for the wealthiest one-fifth of the world compared to the poorest one-fifth went from 30 to 1 in 1960 to 59 to 1 in 1989, according to the U.N. Development Program. It is probably worse today. The technology gap is even greater. While many of us now live and work with computers daily, a majority of the people on the earth, as many as two-thirds by some estimates, have never used a telephone. A swelling population, both in developed and underdeveloped nations, multiplies all these disparities.

The invasion of the desert into productive land can and must be reversed. But it will be less likely to happen when excessive population causes consumption of the greenery that holds the desert at bay. I remember a trip to Senegal, on Africa's west coast, in an area where the desert more and more is encroaching on fertile land. I visited a man whose family sat around him while he talked to me. By his tent, goats were eating the last green growth in the small area. I observed to him that destroying those bushes meant more desert and a harder time for the future. He answered with a shrug, "What can I do? You want me to stop the desert? I want to feed my family. I cannot do both." The more children he had, the more his goats had to support by eating those meager bushes. And the more bushes that disappeared, the more the desert grew.

For an insight into the water vs. population problem, consider a 1996 report that suggests in a decade that Egypt's per capita water supply will be reduced by 30 percent, Niger's by 40 percent, and Kenya's by 50 percent.

Egypt rose from 3 million people in the seventh century B.C. to 20 million in a little more than two centuries. Wars and plagues brought the population down to 7 million, and by the year 541 A.D., the population grew to almost 30 million. But over the next twelve centuries, a series of plagues and two major wars brought the number down to 3 million again in 1950, where it had been 2,000 years before. In the years since then, Egypt's population has jumped to 62 million people—and is still climbing.[5] Wars now take a much smaller percentage of the world's population; health care has improved and prolonged life; and when drought or some other disaster strikes a nation, the world knows about it and usually responds. These developments are good—if we husband the resources to take care of the population, and limit population growth through voluntary family planning.

Economic problems become more severe with population growth. The average income in the Middle East is roughly one-tenth that of Western Europe. Egypt has one-fifth of its workforce unemployed. It is vigorously promoting family planning and healthier practices that over two decades have reduced the infant mortality rate from 170 deaths per 1,000 live births to 85 per 1,000, but that good news also brings problems with it as more people survive and live longer. Egypt adds 1 million people to its total population every ten months.

Lifting educational standards and providing educational opportunities is key to population control. "Education is to population control as desalination is to the water problem," one writer observes.[6] In much of the Middle East, Africa, and Asia, education for girls has been lacking. That is gradually improving, but as late as 1985, only 3 percent of the adult females in the Yemen Arab Republic could read and write. As education for women rises, birth rates fall.

Slowing population growth will help with the water crisis and the less critical but important questions of the economy and the quality of life.

• **What may seem irrelevant, until it is examined, is the state of democracy in the world. Dictatorships tend to have a much worse record of water and air pollution than nations where the public has a strong voice.**

The striking contrast in water and air pollution between East Germany and West Germany existed primarily because one government, West Germany, had to respond to the concerns of people (including a relatively strong Green Party) while East Germany had a dictatorship under which no one had the right to protest miserable conditions and almost nonexistent pollution standards.

When I visited Cracow, Poland, I remember being startled to learn that the people in that area had an average life span six years less than other areas of Poland because of the air pollution coming from the steel mills of Czechoslovakia—on top of Poland's own air pollution, which stemmed from weak environmental standards. Both governments, then dominated by the Soviet Union, could do nothing about it, even if they were so inclined. And public protest was not safe, as it never is under a dictatorship.

There are many Americans concerned about safety in our nuclear power plants, but compared with the Soviet's Chernobyl plant, ours are environmental models. Dictators do not have to deal with letters to the editor or editorials; they do not have to worry about the next election; they do not have to be concerned with what an opposition party might say. And under such a government, when there are standards of pollution that do not protect the public, no prying reporter will get the information or have the right to publish it.

China has serious pollution problems. Beijing has sixteen times as much pollution as New York City. But you can be sure that there will be no protest in Tiananmen Square with citizens carrying placards to urge a change in government policy. That happens only in a free system or one attempting to break free.

When Ethiopia moved from a dictatorship to a democracy the clamor for safe water erupted, and that nation is making progress, even though almost four-fifths of the people there still lack that service.

People in a democracy can demonstrate for piped water and sewers. People living under a dictatorship cannot do it. The story in the previous chapter about people in the *favelas* of Sao Paulo getting safer water and sewers occurred *after* Brazil's military dictatorship fell.

• If the wealthier nations would agree to make greater loan guarantees and grants to the World Bank to assist in bringing piped water and basic sanitation to the poorer nations, the rich and the poor would benefit.

Does anyone really believe that diseases stop at the boundaries of any nation? Ever hear of Asian flu? Ever hear of AIDS? Far too many more examples are available. Does anyone really believe that the world can be stable when many of us enjoy good water and sanitation but are unwilling to sacrifice even a little so that others have these basics? Does anyone believe that a world in crisis over water will result in turmoil and destruction only in the poor nations?

During the entire decade of the 1980s, developing nations spent approximately $133 billion on piped water and sanitation services. *That is one-half of one year's defense budget for the United States.* The World Bank, which loaned about $40 billion of that $133 billion for poorer countries, has never defaulted on a loan to guarantors, and if the wealthier nations could give a combination of loan guarantees plus grants to the World Bank in substantially greater numbers than is now the case, the quality of life and length of life in the poorer nations would improve, and the rest of humanity would be plagued by fewer diseases. It is the humanitarian thing to do. It is also enlightened selfishness.

President Ronald Reagan once suggested that the nations who are more fortunate should devote 1 percent of their national income to helping those less fortunate. Now the United States is devoting less than one-seventh of 1 percent of our national income for that purpose. Under the enlightened and generous Marshall Plan, the United States led the world in economic assistance beyond our borders. Now, in *percentage of our income* devoted to developmental assistance, we are in last place—twenty-first among the twenty-one wealthiest nations. Only Denmark, Norway, the Netherlands, and Saudi Arabia approach the responsible 1 percent figure suggested by our conservative Republican president.

Part of the answer on the looming water crisis will have to be greater distribution of food from the more fortunate nations to the less fortunate nations. That takes place within a nation, such as California fruits and vegetables reaching the tables of Illinois. And it takes place between nations, primarily between wealthier countries. From a purely theoretical viewpoint, this distribution of food within nations and between nations can be of significant help, but the diminishing response of the United States and other nations to world poverty is not likely to be reversed quickly, particularly as food gradually becomes more and more expensive.

I confess to being discouraged when I read that steps to improve water in Namibia in Africa are being financed because Finland is putting in $8 for each $1 that Namibia raises. I applaud the Finns, but I wonder: Where is the leadership from the economic giant of the world?

According to World Bank estimates, Jordan invests 3.7 percent of its national income in water resources; Algeria, Tunisia, and Morocco each 3.1 percent. By comparison, the United States invests a tiny fraction of 1 percent. We have been blessed, but we cannot smugly sit on our huge water resources and ignore the water-poor world.

In addition to our one-seventh of 1 percent that we now spend on assistance to the world's poor, we and other nations should agree to contribute and/or guarantee an extra one-tenth of 1 percent of our national income for one year. For the United

States that would be $70 billion for this purpose, including research on desalination. Everyone in the world would benefit. Sixty billion dollars of the U.S. $70 billion could be a World Bank loan guarantee. The World Bank needs the guarantee to get low interest rates on loans, but—up to this point—our government has never been called upon to "pay up" for a World Bank guarantee. The leadership of the World Bank has been consistently cautious, too cautious in the opinion of some of its critics. A one-time guarantee of $60 billion by us, with other nations following, would make a huge difference in the lives of *billions* of people. Most of the money for water cleanup must come from the developing nations themselves, but they need help. The real question is not the wisdom of doing this; the question is whether we will have leadership with the courage to ask for it, and enough courageous members of Congress to vote for it. If the United States would lead, other nations would follow. It is noteworthy that when the United States cuts back on its commitment to the United Nations and to international developmental assistance, there is also slippage in other nations. At one point under the Marshall Plan, one of the most compassionate and sensible actions in the history of nations, the United States spent 2.9 percent of its national income on helping the poor beyond our borders. Since then our income, adjusted for inflation, has more than doubled, and our assistance has gone down to less than one-fifteenth the former figure.

Has the world's only superpower lost its courage, its vision, its willingness to lead?

We can do better. We must do better. If we look for a cheap way out of the coming crisis, we will pay dearly in dollars and in costs to humanity.

• An International Court for Water must be established to arbitrate disputes between nations when they cannot reach consensus on their own.

The already high number of such disputes will grow, probably dramatically. Like the International Court at the Hague in the Netherlands, an international water court would have no muscle to enforce its decision, but the court at the Hague has been amazingly effective. Nations generally accept the court's verdicts even though they are not compelled to do so.

Because disputes about water will tend to be technical, requiring expertise on the part of the mediating body, a separate court is desirable. It would cost the community of nations almost nothing, and could help avoid major political or armed conflicts.

After writing the above two paragraphs, I came across an article in Northwestern University's *Journal of International Law and Business* that notes: "There is no adequate forum to resolve disputes and apply the principle of international water law. The International Court of Justice . . . lacks the expertise to sufficiently resolve environmental issues and to enforce environmental commitments."[7]

Governments will have to work together more, and there is movement in that direction, everything from the creation of the World Water Council in the United States, an advisory body, to the protocol adopted by the Southern African Development Community nations for cooperation on water to entities like the Western States Water Council. Cooperation is not *the* answer to our problems, but it is part of the answer. The states along the Colorado River provide a domestic example. Cooperation will not solve the long-term problem, but it can alleviate distress that soon will be upon some of the states. Cooperation is politically sensitive and complicated. The legal status of water from state to state is an example: in Colorado, it is privately owned; in Wyoming the state owns the water, and its use requires a state permit; Utah defines water as privately owned, but it cannot be sold across the state border.

Nevada, working with California to construct a concrete canal in the Imperial Valley and getting some of the saved water in return, is an example of the type of cooperation that would harm no one. Some sensible sale or lease of allocated rights of the Colorado River water should be encouraged. If one state has a surplus, and another state has a shortage, why not work out an agreement? The barriers to doing it are both practical and emotional. The practical barriers can be surmounted with carefully drafted understandings. The emotional barriers are greater obstacles. If grim water realities do not move the states to greater cooperation, another specter might. Senator Harry Reid of Nevada, a highly respected and effective legislator, has said matter-of-factly that if the states don't start cooperating more, Congress will have to move in with answers. As the author of one of only two measures ever passed in the history of Congress to force a settlement of a water dispute between states (the other occurring in 1928), Senator Reid speaks with more than usual authority.[8] Thoughtful state leaders may find congressional action a greater threat to their future than unwanted cooperation with a neighboring state. Not many western leaders will want senators from Illinois and New York and other non-western states deciding their fate.

Among nations, cooperation is vital.

That is easy to write, not easily achieved. But it can be achieved. After World War II, I served in the U.S. Army in Coburg, a German city of approximately 40,000. The friends I made there—a newspaper editor, court officials, and others—all assured me that Germany and France would inevitably fight again in another generation because the animosities are so deep-seated, rooted in history and tradition. When I argued with them that this was not inevitable, the one official called me "an idealistic, unrealistic young American." But today no one thinks war between Germany and France is even a remote possibility. Nations can learn to cooperate—and benefit from it. For the Middle East, cooperation and coordination are important to economic development and other important goals, but they are *essential* for the water supply. Turkey, which has not played a constructive role in resolving problems with Cyprus or Armenia, has, however, been a constructive if low-key player in Arab-Israeli matters, or at least was until its change of government in the summer of 1996. The late President Turgut Ozal of Turkey proposed a Peace Water Pipeline that would carry water to all the nations of the area, all the way to Saudi Arabia. A massive $20 billion project, most nations welcomed the idea, but Syria shot it down. And growing water problems in southeastern Turkey increased domestic opposition to the plan. One Turkish leader reacted: "We will have seventy million people by the year 2000, and we will not have enough water for our own people."[9] An Israeli official commented, "A cubic meter of water in Turkey costs nothing, but the cost of transporting it here would be very high. At the end of the day, we shall deal with water in many ways. Desalination, which is getting cheaper all the time, will be the main one."[10] The pipeline idea is not likely to see fruition, but the idea that nations should work together on something like this is sound.

Former United Nations secretary-general Boutros-Ghali illustrates the difficulty of achieving cooperation between nations on water issues: "It is relatively easy to negotiate a treaty to end a conflict between warring parties. But to negotiate a water-sharing treaty, that is a much greater challenge. The war treaty comes after five thousand people have died. The water treaty may save five hundred thousand lives."[11]

A sense of the crisis we will face ought to motivate us to cooperate more.

11

WHAT YOU CAN DO

If those of you who have reached this point in the book will take a minimum of thirty minutes of extra time, you can improve the future of humanity. Literally.

I have no startling answers, but simple, undramatic steps can make a huge difference in how a democracy functions, steps that can determine whether it leads or whether it sputters.

Here is your small agenda:

• Write to your House member and to your Senators urging that greater emphasis and more appropriations be made for finding less expensive ways of desalinating seawater.

The logic of doing this is overwhelming. The interest in it is underwhelming. Write in your words, simply asking for their interest and support. You might mention that you hope they will support Senator Harry Reid of Nevada, who is leading this important effort now.

• In a separate letter, urge them to do something specific legislatively for conservation of water, or reducing its pollution.

Glance through the chapters on conservation, pollution, and population again, and pick one thing that interests you. Write about that.

• Write a letter to the editor of your local newspaper.

Make it reasonably short. Short letters are read more often than long letters, and they are more likely to get published. Letters to the editor are generally read more than editorials—and policy-makers are among those who read them. We need to educate both the public and political leaders to the huge problem we will face, and you can help in that education process. An issue that is hardly visible to most people today must be moved to a place of prominence.

• Send a note to your editor, urging him or her to read this book.

We need some newspaper editors and reporters around the nation who become committed to this subject. One editor committed is better than ten editors mildly interested. If you can afford it, send the editor or reporter a copy of this book or talk to him or her about it.

.   .   .

If you are willing to devote more than thirty minutes to this vital area—and I hope you are—here are some more things that you can do:

• If you are a student, write a term paper on the subject. Work it into one of your classes.

This way you can learn more about the precious commodity of water, and educate your teacher—who in turn may influence other students.

• If you are a teacher, have your students do a paper on the subject.

If we could get 1 percent of the people in the nation concerned about this problem, before a major crisis confronts us, we would get action. Your students can be part of that vital 1 percent.

• Suggest to your local church, synagogue, mosque, or religious center that a discussion group should focus on the water issue for one of its meetings.

This is not only a security and economic issue, it is a moral issue. Most religious organizations have some type of discussion group.

• If there is a Rotary Club or other service club in your area, suggest to the program chair that a discussion on this would be in order and that you would be happy to lead it.

I am not favoring Rotary over other civic groups, but several years ago they sponsored an international conference on the water issue, and in June 1997, their magazine had a cover story on the coming water crisis. Many Rotary Clubs and the Rotary Foundation are sponsoring community water projects in the poorest countries. A presentation by you could elevate their support for sound, and in most cases, inexpensive solutions. Get a copy of that edition of the Rotary magazine from your library, if possible. If your library can't get it for you, write to Rotary International, 1560 Sherman Avenue, Evanston, Illinois 60201, and ask for a copy. Explain why you are asking. Most civic clubs are looking for good and challenging programs and would eagerly accept your offer. If you feel more comfortable talking to the Lions or Kiwanis or American Association of University Women or any other group, do it.

- Ask your local librarian to have a display about water books and articles, and ask the library officials to encourage children to make posters.

Many of the most thoughtful people in your community walk through the doors of that library. They are potential allies in this cause if they become informed. Your library can help.

- Get together some evening with six or eight of your friends in someone's home and have a brainstorming session on how you might help to promote this issue.

If you have reasonably creative people, you will come up with twenty ideas, seventeen of them not very good, but you will have three good ones, things that probably did not occur to me. It has the added merit of getting five to seven more people concerned about the issue.

- Let me know what you are doing. I can spread the word to others.

What you do can inspire others. The most contagious thing in the world is not smallpox or measles or AIDS or the flu, but enthusiasm. When people find they are not alone in this interest, enthusiasm grows. A small handful of people in this nation, which happens to have the dominant role of world leadership, can change this nation and, through it, the world. I want to hear from you. You can reach me by writing to:

Paul Simon
Public Policy Institute
Southern Illinois University
Carbondale, Illinois 62901-4429

.   .   .

I have delivered the message to you. Whether the future of humanity is bright or not rests partially in your hands. A few compassionate, concerned people can make an immense difference for all of humanity. I hope you are one of those few.

NOTES

Chapter 1: An Overview: World Population and Water

1. *Lutheran Book of Worship* (Minneapolis, Minn.: Augsburg, 1978), 122.
2. William Graves, "Introduction," special edition of *National Geographic* (1993).
3. Lester Brown, *State of the World, 1995* (New York: Norton, 1995), 4.
4. David Gleason, "Water: Kader Asmal's Difficult Choice," *Financial Mail*, 1 September 1995.
5. "Dealing with Water Scarcity in the Next Century," Mark Rosegrant, bulletin of the International Food Policy Research Institute, Washington, D.C.
6. "The Last Drops," Eugene Linden, *Time*, 20 August 1990.
7. "Wally N'Dow," an interview with Robin Wright, *Los Angeles Times*, 5 June 1996.
8. Brownen Maddox, "The World's Tap Seizes Up," *Financial Times*, 17 March 1993.
9. John Rowley, "Running out of Water," *People and the Planet*, no. 2 (1993). Rowley uses the figure ninety nations, but another author in the same publication, Mikael Arnestrand ("Defining Scarcity"), uses the lower number, sixty-five.
10. Daniel Butler, "Water: The Next Source of Trouble," *Worldlink* (November-December 1995).
11. Niveen Tadros, "Shrinking Water Resources: The National Security Issue of [The Next] Century," *Northwestern Journal of International Law and Business* (winter-spring 1996–1997).
12. John Bullein, *The Bulwarke Against All Sickness*, 1562, quoted by H. L. Mencken, *A New Dictionary of Quotations* (New York: Knopf, 1966), 1275.
13. 4 October 1995, Federal News Reuters Transcription Services.
14. *State of New Jersey* v. *State of New York*, 283 U.S. 336, 342 (1931).
15. Rachel Carson, *Silent Spring* (Boston: Houghton Mifflin, 1987), 39.
16. Paul and Anne Ehrlich, *Population Explosion* (New York: Simon and Schuster, 1990), 28.
17. Peter Gleick, address to the National Press Club, 5 April 1995.
18. These are conservative UNICEF figures. The United Nations Environment

Programme places the figure much higher, at 25,000 a day. An article in *Foreign Policy* places it at 40,000.

19. "The Cost of Dirty Water," *People and the Planet*, no. 2 (1993).

20. Klaus Lanz, *Greenpeace Book of Water* (New York: Sterling, 1995), 21.

21. Mary Cooper, "Global Water Shortages," *Congressional Quarterly Researcher*, 15 December 1995.

22. Sandra Postel, "Forging a Sustainable Water Strategy," in *State of the World: 1996*, Lester Brown, ed. (New York: Norton, 1996), 44.

23. World Resources Institute, quoted in Robert Engelman and Pamela LeRoy, *Sustaining Water* (Washington: Population Action International, 1993), 11.

24. Samuel Taylor Coleridge, "The Rime of the Ancient Mariner," *Oxford Dictionary of Quotations*, 2nd ed. (London: Oxford University Press, 1955), 149.

25. Dirk Johnson, "Weed Killers in Tap Water in Corn Belt," *New York Times*, 18 August 1995.

26. Report of Ismail Serageldin, Vice President, World Bank, to the Fifth Stockholm Water Symposium, 7 August 1995.

27. *Socialist Industry* (June 1989), quoted in Daniel Hillel, *Out of the Earth*, (New York: Free Press, 1991), 156.

28. Stephen Kinzer, "Only Water, Maybe, But It Was a People's Lifeblood," *New York Times*, 28 October 1997.

29. Sandra Postel, "Where Have All the Rivers Gone?", *World Watch* (May-June 1995).

30. Niu Mao Sheng, quoted in Lester R. Brown, "Nature's Limits," in *State of the World 1995*, Linda Starke, ed. (New York: Norton, 1995), 18.

Chapter 2: California

1. Peter Gleick, Penn Loh, Santos Gomez, and Jason Morrison, *California Water 2020: A Sustainable Vision* (Oakland: Pacific Institute, 1995), ES 1. Part of the information in this chapter comes from this excellent report.

2. Marc Reisner, *Cadillac Desert* (New York: Penguin, 1986), 344–345.

3. Engineer's Report, Metropolitan Water District of Southern California (January 1995), 2.

4. *Los Angeles Times*, Washington Edition, 19 May 1995.

5. Quoted in James Sterngold, "A Blow for Water Independence," *New York Times*, 6 August 1996.

6. *California Water 2020*, ES 6.

7. Phil Garlington, "Regional Report: Desert Dweller Fights for Lake," *Orange County Register*, 29 June 1997.

8. William Booth, "Los Angeles Water May Reverse Flow," *Washington Post*, 16 May 1997.

9. California officials use the 50 percent or higher figure. The U.S. Bureau of Reclamation says it is slightly less than 40 percent. Both statistics show the southern part of the state heavily dependent on the Colorado River.

10. "Water for Southern California," pamphlet published by Metropolitan Water District of Southern California, 1994.
11. Reisner, op. cit., 126–127.

Chapter 3: Las Vegas

1. Ernie Pyle, "Nevada Old and New," in *Travels in the Americas*, Jack Newcome, ed. (New York: Weidenfeld and Nicolson, 1989), 139.
2. Everett Jesse, *State of Nevada, Forecast of County, Municipal and Industrial Water Needs* (Carson City: Department of Conservation and Natural Resources, 1992), 6–8.
3. Patricia Mulroy, quoted in Melissa Healy, "Interior Department Aims to Rechannel Water Policy in West," *Los Angeles Times*, 19 September 1994.
4. Steve LaRue, "Wagering for Water," *San Diego Union-Tribune*, 31 July 1995.
5. Francis Griffith Newlands, quoted in Marc Reisner, *Cadillac Desert* (New York: Penguin, 1986), 116.
6. Eric Garner and Michelle Ouellette, "Future Shock? The Law of the Colorado River in the Twenty-First Century," *Arizona State Law Journal* (Summer 1995).
7. David Rosenbaum, "Las Vegas Area Slakes Its Thirst," *Engineering News-Record* 10 (April 1995).
8. Philip Fradkin, "The River Revisited," *Los Angeles Times Magazine*, 29 October 1995.
9. Tom Jensen, "The Law of the Colorado River: Carefully Planning to Drive off the Cliff," *Water Strategist* (October, 1994).
10. Quoted by Nevada Deputy Attorney General Peggy Twedt in an undated 1992 statement.
11. Ibid.
12. *State of Arizona* v. *State of California*, 376 U.S. 340 (1964).
13. While lining canals with concrete or plastic does save sizable amounts of water, it is not an unmixed blessing. Unlined canals and ditches return water to the soil, some of which eventually replenishes underground aquifers.
14. Ken Leiser, "Las Vegas, MWD Water Deal Comes up Empty," *San Diego Union-Tribune*, 20 March 1996.
15. Steve LaRue, "Officials Hope to Head off State Water War," *San Diego Union-Tribune*, 24 December 1995.
16. "Water-Banking Legislation Charting out Destiny," editorial, *Arizona Republic*, 8 February 1996.
17. Quoted in Elliot Diringer, "Warning Signs of New War over Water," *San Francisco Chronicle*, 11 January 1994.
18. Ibid.
19. Martin Van Der Werf, "Symington Asks Nevada to Curb Growth," *Arizona Republic*, 28 June 1995.
20. John Gunther, *Inside U.S.A.* (New York: Harper, 1947), 215.

21. Susan Greene and Mary Hynes, "Southern Nevada's New Paradigm for Water Management," *Las Vegas Review Journal*, 13 October 1996.

Chapter 4: Florida and Other States

1. Paul and Anne Ehrlich, *The Population Explosion* (New York: Simon and Schuster, 1990) 131–132.
2. Albert Gore Jr., *Earth in the Balance* (New York: Plume, 1992), 73.
3. *Florida Water Plan*, adopted 8 December 1995 (Florida Department of Environmental Protection), 1.
4. Quoted in "Area Needs Strategy for Water, Panel Says," *St. Petersburg Times*, 20 April 1995.
5. Mark Farrell, letter to Paul Simon, 3 May 1995.
6. Sylvia Earle, *Sea Change* (New York: Putnam's, 1995), 226–227.
7. Ted Williams, quoted in Teresa Burney, "Critics Find Fault in Water Pact," *St. Petersburg Times*, 22 July 1995.
8. Ibid., 3.
9. Karen Weintraub, "Major Step Forward for Pipeline," *Norfolk Virginian-Pilot*, 21 January 1995.
10. *State of North Carolina* v. *FERC*, 112 F.3d 1175 (DC Cir., 1997).
11. Ibid.
12. Tom Kenworthy, "Mining Industry Labors to Drown Montana Water Quality Initiative," *Washington Post*, 30 October 1997.
13. Donald Hare, state director of Rural Economic and Community Development, letter to John Romano, USDA, 10 January 1996.
14. Ellen King Huntoon, report to John Romano, USDA, 28 August 1995.
15. James Bays, letter to John Romano, USDA, 17 August 1995.
16. Karl Ross, "Island's Oases Become Its Water Tanker Trucks," *Washington Post*, 4 September 1994.
17. Bobby Lewis, West Virginia director, Rural Economic and Community Development, letter to John Romano, USDA, 15 August 1995.
18. 16 July 1996, quoted in "Water 2000," pamphlet distributed by the U.S. Department of Agriculture (October 1997), 6.
19. Paul Kennedy, *Preparing for the Twenty-First Century* (New York: Random House, 1993), 319–320.
20. Erla Zwingle, "Wellspring of the High Plains," *National Geographic* (March 1993).
21. Report of Dan Pearson and Craig Pedersen to Lt. Governor Bob Bullock, 30 August 1996.
22. Mike Personett, letter to Paul Simon, 26 September 1996.
23. Marc Reisner, *Cadillac Desert* (New York: Penguin, 1986), 10–11.

Chapter 5: The Middle East

1. Koran, Al-Anbiya 30.
2. Jeffrey Berkoff, *A Strategy for Managing Water in the Middle East and North Africa* (Washington: World Bank, 1994), xi.
3. Priit J. Vesilind, "The Middle East's Critical Resource: Water," *National Geographic* (May 1993).
4. Boutros-Ghali interview with Joyce Starr, in Joyce Starr, *Covenant Over Middle Eastern Waters* (New York: Henry Holt, 1995), 47.
5. Starr, *op. cit.*
6. Vesilind, *op. cit.*
7. Ibid.
8. Warren Christopher, "American Diplomacy and the Global Environmental Challenges of the 21st Century," *Renewable Resources Journal* (spring 1996).
9. Conversation with Paul Simon, 14 August 1996.
10. Aaron Wolf, "Middle East Water Conflicts and Directions for Conflict Resolution" (discussion paper, International Food Policy Research Institute, Washington, March 1996).
11. Shimon Peres, *The New Middle East* (New York: Henry Holt, 1993), 123–124.
12. Quoted in Daniel Butler, "Water: The Next Source of Trouble," *World Link* (November-December 1995).
13. Jessica Matthews, "Population vs. Peace," *Washington Post*, 3 June 1996.
14. James Moore, "Parting the Waters: Calculating Israeli and Palestinian Entitlements," *Middle East Policy* 3 (1994).
15. Jeremy Berkoff, *A Strategy for Managing Water in the Middle East and North Africa* (Washington: World Bank, 1994), 63.
16. Jay Bushinsky, "Water Shortage Threatens Middle East," *Chicago Sun-Times*, 7 July 1995.
17. Quoted in Vesilind, "The Middle East's Critical Resource: Water."
18. Abd Fattah Miski, quoted in Barbara Nimri Aziz, "Syria's Water Solution," *Toward Freedom* (June-July 1995).
19. Quoted in Sandra Postel, "The Politics of Water," *World Watch* (July-August 1993).
20. Mahmoud Abu-Zeid, chairman of the Egyptian Water Research Center, quoted in Vesilind, "The Middle East's Critical Resource: Water."
21. Thomas Naff and Ruth Matson, *Water in the Middle East: Conflict or Cooperation?* (Univ. of Pennsylvania: Middle East Research Institute, 1984), 46.
22. Quoted in Warren Christopher, "American Diplomacy and the Global Environmental Challenges of the 21st Century," *Renewable Resource Journal* (spring 1996).
23. Bruce Stutz, "Water and Peace," *Audubon* (September-October 1994).
24. *Jerusalem Post*, 7 May 1995, quoted in *The Jerusalem Insider*, 22 July 1996.
25. An excellent discussion of Israel's water and sewage problem is in a paper by

Yossi Laster, "The Political Economy of Waste Water in Israel" (Jerusalem: Institute for Advanced Strategic and Political Studies, 1996).

26. Felice Maranz, "Too Little Water Leaves Israelis Stoned," *Jerusalem Report*, 6 May 1993.
27. Judy Peres, "In Parched West Bank, Valuable Water Ignites Latest Fight," *Chicago Tribune*, 13 August 1995.
28. Peres, *The New Middle East*, 132.

Chapter 6: Other Nations

1. Sandra Postel, "Forging a Sustainable Water Strategy," in *State of the World, 1996*, Lester Brown, ed. (New York: Norton, 1996), 40.
2. Patrick E. Tyler, "China's Fickle Rivers: Dry Farms, Needy Industry Bring a Water Crisis," *New York Times*, 23 May 1996.
3. Arthur Conacher, "Salt of the Earth," *Environment* (July-August 1990).
4. Paul and Anne Ehrlich, *The Population Explosion* (New York: Simon and Schuster, 1990), 154.
5. Sanjay Mohanty, "Overdevelopment and Sustainability of Groundwater Resources in India: A Case-Study," *Proceedings of the IDA World Congress on Desalination and Water Sciences*, vol. 2 (Abu Dhabi: UAE University, 1995), 513–525.
6. *International Security* (Summer 1993).
7. "Cyprus Launches Water Saving Campaign," Xinhua News Agency, 27 June 1996.
8. Much of this information comes from *Greece: A Country Study*, Glenn Curtis, ed. (Washington: Library of Congress, 1994).
9. C. A. Pappas, "Water Supply and Desalination in Greece," *Desalination and Water Reuse*, vol. 4, no. 2.
10. "Water and Conflict: Fresh Water Resources and International Security," *International Security* (summer 1993).
11. "Liquidity Crises," *The Economist*, 14 November 1992.
12. Address by Joyce R. Starr, published in "Briefing Book for the African Water Summit," 24–27 June 1990.
13. Study by D. A. Mashauri, quoted in *Water Resources Management in Tanzania*, Rafik Hirji and Francois-Marie Patorni, eds. (Washington: World Bank, 1994), 64.
14. David Gleason, "Kader Asmal's Difficult Choices," *Financial Mail*, 1 September 1996.
15. Data in Tony Hodges, *Western Sahara* (Westport, Conn.: Lawrence Hill, 1983).
16. "Shivute Delivers Pentecost Lecture," *Wittenberg Today* 1 (1995).
17. Bronwen Maddox, "Demand for Fresh Water Is Growing Worldwide as the Supply Is Drying Up," *London Financial Times* (undated clipping, possibly April 1993).
18. John Hooper, "Environment: The Drain on Spain," *The Guardian*, 14 June 1995.

19. *Ecological Security & Canada's Freshwater Resources* (Ottawa: Rawson Academy of Aquatic Science, 1992), 4.
20. Ibid., 9.

Chapter 7: Desalination

1. Dwight Eisenhower, "A Proposal for Our Time," *Reader's Digest* (June 1968).
2. Public Papers of the Presidents: Dwight D. Eisenhower, 1960 (Washington: Government Printing Office, 1961), 410.
3. Thomas Jefferson, Report to Congress, *Jefferson Cyclopedia*, John Foley, ed. (New York: Funk and Wagnalls, 1900), 971.
4. Aristotle, Meteorologica, *The Complete Works of Aristotle*, Jonathan Barnes, ed., vol. 1 (Princeton: Princeton University Press, 1984), 580.
5. Remarks spoken for the dedication of a Texas conversion plant. By telephone speaker, 21 June 1961. *Speeches of Senator John F. Kennedy: Presidential Campaign of 1960* (Washington: U.S. Government Printing Office, 1961), 334–335.
6. Ibid., 22 September 1960.
7. James Mielke, "Desalination: Meeting a Growing Need," *CRS Review* (December 1991).
8. Editorial, "No More B-2s," *St. Louis Post-Dispatch*, 6 September 1997.
9. Leon Awerbuch, letter to Paul Simon, 18 January 1996.
10. Leon Awerbuch, testimony before the House Subcommittee on Science, 17 July 1991 (Washington: U.S. Government Printing Office, 1992), 167.
11. John Briscoe, Chief, Water and Sanitation Division in the Transportation, Water and Urban Development Department, World Bank, conversation with Paul Simon, 29 August 1995.
12. Joyce Starr, "Water Wars," *Foreign Policy* (spring 1991).
13. Neil Stessman, testimony, Senate Subcommittee on Forests and Public Land Management, 13 December 1995.
14. Charles H. Duell, quoted in "The Past, Imperfect," *Newsweek*, 15 July 1966.
15. Hearing report of Subcommittee on Irrigation and Reclamation, U.S. House of Representatives, 27 April 1971, p. 30.
16. *Proceedings of the International Desalination Association World Congress* (Abu Dhabi: UAE University, 1995), vol. 2, inside back cover.
17. *Cyprus* (Nicosia: Cypriot Government, 1994), 94.
18. Quoted in "The Past, Imperfect," *Newsweek*, 15 July 1996.
19. Ross Gelbspan, *The Heat Is On* (Reading, Mass.: Addison-Wesley, 1997), 2.
20. Jessica Matthews, "In Denial About Global Warming," *Washington Post*, 29 January 1996.
21. George Mitchell, *World on Fire* (New York: Scribner's, 1991), 83.
22. John Cushman Jr., "U.S. Emits Greenhouse Gases at the Highest Rate in Years," *New York Times*, 21 October 1997.
23. Leon Awerbuch, letter to Paul Simon, 21 October 1997.

24. Gregg Easterbrook, "Here Comes the Sun," *New Yorker,* 10 April 1995.
25. Advertisement of Weizmann Institute, *New York Times,* 11 March 1997.
26. Article by Julie Edelson Halpert, *New York Times,* 5 June 1996.
27. Yusuf Hamud, M. H. El-Banhawy, and Bushara Ahmad, "The Economical Aspects of Using Solar Energy for the Rural Areas of the Arabian Gulf," *Proceedings of the International Desalination Congress* (Abu Dhabi: UAE University, 1995), 361.
28. Chris Fay, quoted in Jessica Matthews, "Energy Efficiency: Waste Not, Want Less," *Washington Post,* 15 July 1996.
29. Undated clipping, interview with the *New York Times.*
30. Most scientists disagree with me on this. My assumption is that over time we will reduce the cost of desalination dramatically so that eventually there will be a thousand times as much use of desalination than is now the case. That would have a measurable effect on the ocean level, though not a large impact.
31. Holly Stoerker, letter to Paul Simon, 11 June 1996.
32. Quoted in George Mitchell, *World on Fire* (New York: Scribner's, 1991), 177.
33. Mitchell, op. cit., 131.
34. Committee on Policy Implications of Greenhouse Warming, *Policy Implications of Greenhouse Warming* (Washington: National Academy Press, 1992), 12.
35. Avishay Braverman, Nehemiah Hassid, and Shalom Drori, "Desalination Prospects West of the Jordan River," International Desalination Association, *Report of World Congress* 2 (1995), 606.
36. Shimon Peres, *The New Middle East* (New York: Henry Holt, 1993), 131–132.
37. Yitzhak Rabin, in conversation with Kurt Stehling, as told by Kurt Stehling to Paul Simon, 29 March 1996.
38. Aaron Wolf, "Water for Peace in the Jordan River Watershed," *Natural Resources Journal* (Summer 1993).
39. Sultan Qaboos Bin Said Al Said, interview by Anne Joyce of *Middle East Policy,* in *Water* (April 1995).
40. Mohammed H. Al-Attar et al., "Kuwait Institute for Scientific Research," *Desalination & Water Reuse* (November-December 1995).
41. Osama A. El Masry, "On the Selection and Optimization of Cogeneration Plants for Egypt," *International Desalination World Congress Proceedings* 3 (Abu Dhabi Printing and Publishing, 1995), 413.
42. *California Water 2020,* 96.
43. "Seawater Desalination Demonstration Project," brochure by the Metropolitan Water District of Southern California (October 1994), 1.
44. Brad Hiltscher, testimony, Subcommittee on Energy and Development, U.S. House of Representatives, 22 March 1995.
45. Srwer Iman and Shahnaz Fatima, "Hazardous Effects of Desalinated Water on Human Lives and Plant Lives and Their Remedies," *Proceedings of the IDA World Congress on Desalination* (United Arab Emirates University: Abu Dhabi, 1995), vol. 2, 547.
46. Dr. Kurt Stehling, conversation with Paul Simon, 29 March 1996.

47. *Seawater Desalination* (Brooksville, Fla.: Southwest Florida Water Management District, 1995), 1.
48. Ibid., 6.
49. Story by Victor Hull, *Sarasota Herald-Tribune*, 8 May 1995.
50. Quoted in David Pedreira, "No Relief in Sight for Wellfields," *Tampa Tribune*, 21 July 1995.
51. Mark Farrell, letter to Paul Simon, 3 May 1995.
52. Jonathon Jones, "Desalination Holds Promise in Lower Rio Grande Valley," *American Desalting Association News* (May-June 1996).
53. Aller Stikker, letter to Paul Simon, 21 May 1996.
54. Christopher Lant, memorandum to Paul Simon, 13 October 1997.
55. Klaus Lanz, *The Greenpeace Book of Water* (New York: Sterling, 1995), 29.
56. Mark Farrell, "Seawater Desalination in Florida," *International Desalination and Water Reuse Quarterly* (May-June 1996).
57. Richard Probst, "The Virginia Beach Quest for Water: Drowning in a Sea of Litigation," *Brigham Young University Journal of Public Law* (1997).
58. Priit Vesilind, "The Middle East's Critical Resource: Water," *National Geographic* (May 1993).
59. Peres, *The New Middle East*, 90.
60. Joyce Starr, interview with David Hulme, 28 June 1990.

Chapter 8: The Big Short-Term Payoff: Conservation

1. Sandra Postel, *Last Oasis* (New York: Norton, 1992), 23.
2. *Desalination Research*, hearing transcript, Subcommittee on Science, 17 July 1991 (Washington: U.S. Government Printing Office: 1992), 1.
3. Jeanne McDowell and Richard Woodbury, "A Fight over Liquid Gold," *Time*, 22 July 1991.
4. Quoted in Raymond Meier and Jon Bowermaster, "Dire Straits: Water as an Endangered Resource," *Harper's Bazaar*, July 1993.
5. Leslie Spencer, "Water: The West's Most Misallocated Resource," *Forbes*, 27 April 1992.
6. Terry Anderson, "Water Options for the Blue Planet," *The True State of the Planet*, Ronald Bailey, ed. (New York: Free Press, 1995), 268–273.
7. Ibid., 268.
8. Ibid., 269–270.
9. Christopher Lant, chair, Geography Department, Southern Illinois University, Carbondale, memorandum to Paul Simon, 13 October 1997.
10. Ismail Serageldin, "Toward Sustainable Management of Water Resources," booklet published by the World Bank, 1995, 5.
11. Al Kamen, "Free Grass for Life," *Washington Post*, 20 September 1995.
12. Postel, ibid., 138.
13. Mark Rosegrant, "Water Resources in the 21st Century," paper presented at a conference in Japan, International Food Policy Research Institute (1995), 7.

14. *California Water 2020*, 4.
15. Notes of Arthur Simon, 8 October 1997.
16. Karl Ross, "Island's Oases Become Its Water Tanker Trucks," *Washington Post*, 4 September 1994. Also "For Second Time in Three Years, Water Rationed in San Juan," *New York Times*, 22 June 1997.
17. Sandra Postel, "The Politics of Water," *World Watch* (July-August 1993).
18. Everett Jesse, *State of Nevada, Forecast of County, Municipal and Industrial Water Needs* (Carson City: Department of Conservation and Natural Resources, 1992), 30.
19. Joyce Starr, *Covenant over Middle Eastern Waters* (New York: Henry Holt, 1995), 82.
20. Gail Bingham, Aaron Wolf, and Tim Wohlgenant, *Resolving Water Disputes* (Washington: AID, 1994), 93.
21. Adnan Akkad, "Conservation in the Arabian Gulf Countries," *Journal of the American Water Works Association* (May 1990).
22. Daniel Butler, "Water: The Next Source of Trouble," *World Link* (November-December 1995).
23. Story by Paul Valentine, *Washington Post*, 12 May 1996.
24. Richard Raines, "Following the Law in Idaho: Legal and Institutional Impediments to Conjunctive Water Management," *Water Resources* (winter 1997).
25. Mike Personett, E-mail to Paul Simon, 30 May 1997.
26. Erla Zwingle, "Wellspring of the High Plains," *National Geographic* (March 1993).
27. Marc Reisner, *Cadillac Desert* (New York: Penguin, 1986), 454.

Chapter 9: Pollution Complicates Everything

1. Nicholas Kristof, *New York Times*, 9 January 1997.
2. Paul Salopek, *Chicago Tribune*, 15 December 1996.
3. Nicholas Kristof, "For Third World, Water Is Still a Deadly Drink," *New York Times*, 9 January 1997.
4. Joyce Starr, *Covenant over Middle Eastern Waters* (New York: Holt, 1995), 139.
5. "Largest Man-Made Lakes Going to Waste," *Washington Post*, 24 November 1995.
6. Michael Weber and Judith Gradwohl, *The Wealth of Oceans* (New York: Norton, 1995), 161.
7. *Florida Water Plan 1995* (Tallahassee: Department of Environmental Protection, 1995), 24.
8. Isabel Blackett, *Low-Cost Urban Sanitation in Lesotho* (Washington: World Bank, 1994), 17.
9. Gregg Easterbrook, "Here Comes the Sun," *New Yorker,* 10 April 1995.
10. 9 April 1996, address in *Renewable Resources Journal* (spring 1996).
11. Madeleine Nash, "The Fish Crisis," *Newsweek*, 11 August 1997.
12. Weber and Gradwohl, ibid., 152.

13. Daniel Sitarz, *Agenda 21* (Carbondale, Ill.: Earth Press, 1994), 21.
14. Quoted in Michael Lemonick, "The Last Frontier," *Time*, 14 August 1995.

Chapter 10: Dealing with Population and . . .

1. Quoted in Michael Weber and Judith Gradwohl, *The Wealth of Oceans* (New York: Norton, 1995), 199.
2. Within religious groups there are exceptions. In what many term the ultra-orthodox in the Jewish community in Jerusalem, for example, the average family has 8.9 children.
3. *1995 Care Annual Report*, 10–11.
4. Figures supplied by the Population Institute, Washington, D.C.
5. A good discussion of population trends over the centuries is in Joel Cohen, *How Many People Can the Earth Support?* (New York: Norton, 1995), 28–42.
6. Thomas McDermott, letter to Paul Simon, 14 October 1997.
7. Niveen Tadros, "Shrinking Water Resources: The National Security Issue of [The Next] Century," *Northwestern Journal of International Law and Business* (winter-spring 1996–1997).
8. The measure settled a dispute between California and Nevada involving the waters of the Truckee and Carson Rivers and Lake Tahoe. *The Stanford Environmental Law Journal* (January 1995) contains details about this legislation and the need for greater congressional involvement in water policy disputes, written by E. Leif Reid, a son of the senator.
9. Foreign Minister Sefa Giray, quoted in Joyce Starr, *Covenant over Middle Eastern Waters* (New York: Henry Holt, 1995), 116.
10. An unidentified Israeli leader, quoted in Eric Silver, "The Ottoman Express," *The Jerusalem Report*, 1 December 1994.
11. Joyce Starr, *Covenant over Middle Eastern Waters* (New York: Henry Holt, 1995), 165–166.

INDEX

194